Syntax and Piagetian Operational Thought

A Developmental Study of Bilingual Children

Ruth V. Tremaine

Georgetown University Press, Washington, D.C. 20057

LIBRARY OF CONGRESS CATALOGING IN PUBLICATION DATA

Tremaine, Ruth V.   1941-
    Syntax and Piagetian operational thought

    Includes bibliographical references.
    1. Children--Language. 2. Bilingualism. 3. Learning,
Psychology of. 4. Grammar, Comparative and general--
Syntax. 5. Piaget, Jean, 1896-   I. Title. [DNLM: 1. Child
development. 2. Language development. 3. Learning.
LB1139. L3 T789s]
P118.T73   401'.9   75-5749

International Standard Book Number: 0-87840-161-X

CONTENTS

LIST OF TABLES

LIST OF FIGURES

FOREWORD

Serious inquiry into the development of language in children quickly leads to questions regarding the development of cognition. Questions multiply and the problem becomes compounded when language acquisition is bilingual, or bi-systemic. Processes by which the child becomes bilingual challenge the theories of linguistic science and developmental psychology to the cutting edge of those disciplines. Search of the literature reveals few studies which grapple with the bilingual child's acquisition of his two language systems together with his cognitive development in a detailed, empirical approach.

In her study of the interrelationship between language and cognitive development, Ruth Tremaine draws upon the current research of two disciplines-- linguistics and psychology. Focusing on one kind of mental activity, operational processes, Dr. Tremaine argues provocatively and convincingly for the unifying role of Jean Piaget's equilibration model in the acquisition of linguistic as well as cognitive structures. The mechanisms of assimilation and accommodation involved in the development of logico-mathematical reasoning reach far towards accounting for the child's gradual construction of adult grammars. The close relationship between acquisition of operational intelligence and the structures of two languages in the bilingual child permits articulation of a theory converging language acquisition and intelligence.

A theory treating the child's acquisition of knowledge should have applications for what might be done to facilitate that acquisition. Dr. Tremaine's work holds implications for interdisciplinary studies in linguistics, psychology, sociology, and education, with special reference to bilingual education. The findings reported in this work, with its careful methodological procedures and rigorous statistical analyses, make a substantive contribution to the kind of research needed in developmental psycholinguistics today.

Carolyn Kessler
Immaculata College of Washington
Washington, D. C.

ACKNOWLEDGMENTS

To Carolyn Kessler, whose ideas, research, and personal encouragement sparked and sustained the efforts reported herein I am most grateful.

I would like to thank my former professor at the University of Ottawa, Henry P. Edwards, for his support and valuable criticisms throughout the investigation, and Theresa Szyrynski for insightful consultations during the data-gathering phase and later, when interpreting the findings.

Special thanks are extended to the Ottawa Roman Catholic Separate School Board for allowing access to the children of St. Andrew's School, Ottawa, and to the staff of the school for their cheerful co-operation.

The study was undertaken with the financial assistance of the Canada Council.

R. V. T.

INTRODUCTION

The often-discussed problem of how language and thought are related has recently come into sharp focus in the area of developmental psychology. In the last decade, a great deal of research activity has centered around child language acquisition, and yet most workers in the field would agree that the processes by which children learn their first language are still poorly understood. Even less understood are the processes of second language acquisition. The learning principles proposed by behaviorist psychologists have been persuasively attacked, while many researchers find the more recently proposed Cartesian explanations of the language learning process to be just as unsatisfactory.

This study was based on the observation that Piagetian operational thought and the comprehension of syntax develop in remarkably similar ways in young children. This similarity becomes especially evident when syntax is defined in terms of case grammar theory.[1] By investigating the simultaneous development of these two aspects of human ability, it was hoped that some light could be thrown on child bilingualism and on the language learning process in general.

The primary aim of the study was to investigate the possibility that Piagetian operational thought and the comprehension of syntax are based on the same kind of learning process. More specifically, it tested the hypothesis that the attainment of concrete operations would be accompanied by major progress in the comprehension of both English and French syntax by bilingual children. The secondary aims of the study were to describe the development and interrelation of the syntax of two languages when one language is weaker than the other, to partially replicate, using English-French bilingual children, the study done by Kessler (1971) of English-Italian bilingual children, and to test a hypothesis derived from Lambert and Tucker's (1972) suggestion that learning a second language during childhood can facilitate competence in the native language.

NOTE

1. See Appendix A for a general discussion of case grammar.

CHAPTER ONE

THEORETICAL FOCUS

This chapter is organized around the exposition of a particular theoretical outlook on the relationship of language to thought which is emerging in developmental psycholinguistics and related disciplines. The literature discussed below was selected in order to clarify this theoretical position and to explore the possibilities it presents for research.

First, the literature on child bilingualism is briefly summarized, as well as theoretical notions on how a second language is learned. The review then forks into two related aspects of child development, first-language acquisition and the development of logico-mathematical reasoning, in order to show how the most recent research in both fields converges in a similar theoretical outlook. A crucial study by Kessler (1971), which exemplified this theoretical convergence and provided the methodological bases of the present study, is described in detail. Finally, the problems investigated in the study are placed in a theoretical context.

Studies of child bilingualism

Several reviews, summaries, and annotated bibliographies of the extensive literature on child bilingualism are available (Peal and Lambert 1962, Yamamoto 1964, Macnamara 1967, Ching 1969). These studies have been most heterogeneous--in the languages studied, the age groups of the children, the socioeconomic characteristics of the subjects' families, the measures used for assessing degree of language development, intelligence, and school achievement. One of the major questions investigated by these studies was whether knowing a second language adversely affects intellectual development and school achievement. The findings are contradictory in many respects. Some studies found that monolingual children scored higher on measures of intelligence and achievement, some found that they scored lower, and others found that there was no difference between the groups. When psycholinguistic abilities and level of language development were measured, it was usually in terms of vocabulary items, auditory discrimination, reading, and spelling--measures which, in terms of the first-language acquisition studies to be discussed below, are entirely inadequate to assess knowledge of a language.

Longitudinal studies done in Canada on French-English child bilingualism are more relevant to the present study (Barik and Swain 1972, Lambert and

Tucker 1972, Edwards and Casserly 1973). The major motivation behind these studies was to assess whether any educational retardation results from instructing English-speaking children entirely in French, starting at the Grade 1 level. Measures of language development used in these studies were psychometric in nature, and not designed to investigate the underlying processes of language acquisition, either of the first or the second language (e.g. word associations, Illinois Test of Psycholinguistic Abilities [ITPA], Metropolitan Achievement Tests, story ratings, word counts of parts of speech). The results of these studies were similar. In general, no retardation of the French immersion group was found when intelligence and achievement was measured by standardized tests in both languages. As expected, the French immersion children were markedly superior in French language skills, although, after two years of French immersion, they tended to lag behind non-immersion children on measures of English spelling and reading. There was also some indication that following a French immersion program facilitated certain mathematical skills as well as English psycholinguistic skills as measured by the ITPA. Edwards and Casserly (1973:94) concluded that, apart from reading and spelling, 'increased working exposure by basically Anglophone children to a second language benefits not only the acquisition of the second language but also the development of the mother tongue.'

Due to the nature of the measures used in these longitudinal studies, no conclusions could be reached about second language learning strategies. However, it was often noted with astonishment how easily the immersion children transferred skills learned through the medium of the French language to tests conducted in English. Lambert and Tucker (1972) suggested that this transfer of skills between languages may have been due to a more abstract form of learning independent of the language of training.

Regarding the process of second language learning, these authors speculated that a form of 'incipient contrastive linguistics' is practiced by children. That is, when a child is exposed to a second language, he compares the vocabulary and syntax of the two languages and actively searches for equivalents which he does not know. This translation and search process would not only allow him to learn his second language, but would also increase the knowledge of his first one (Lambert and Tucker 1972:207-211).

Lambert and Tucker's speculations on the strategies used by children to learn a second language have some superficial similarities to the contrastive analysis theory of adult second language learning. One version of this theory, based on interference theory in verbal learning experiments, states that adults learn a second language by transferring the known structures of the first one, and where the structures differ between languages, predictable errors will be made ('interference') during the learning process. The validity of this theory has been questioned by both verbal learning psychologists (Tulving and Madigan 1970) and psycholinguists concerned with adult foreign language learning (Jakobovits 1970). This type of contrastive analysis, however, seems to be valid in predicting phonological errors, but not necessarily syntactic errors (Richards 1971).

Another version of contrastive analysis theory is based not on psychological learning experiments but on transformational grammar and rests on the assumption that all languages are the same at their most abstract level (deep structure). Languages differ in the realization of these linguistic universals into surface structure and the task of contrastive analysis is seen to be the identification of contrasted realization rules between languages. Although this approach is mostly at the level of theory nowadays, some successful attempts have been made to demonstrate its analytic usefulness (e.g. Kessler 1969).

Nonetheless, both versions of contrastive analysis theory suggest that, where languages differ, errors will occur during the learning process due to transferring native language patterns onto the second language. Differences between the contrastive analysis theory for adults and Lambert and Tucker's speculations regarding children should be noted at this point. Lambert and Tucker have implied that comparisons and 'transfer' are reciprocal between languages, resulting in broader knowledge of both languages. In other words, the learning effects in children do not occur only in one direction from the native language to the second language.

An alternative theory of second language learning by children has come from research on first-language acquisition. This theory has been called the L2=L1 hypothesis (Dulay and Burt 1972). Briefly, it states that structural errors made by children below the age of puberty while learning a second language (L2) will resemble the types of errors they simultaneously make in the continued learning of their first language (L1). In other words, the types of errors made in both languages will reflect the developmental level of the child, and will not be due to 'interference' by an already known L1 structure. Dulay and Burt (1972) noted with dismay the absence of comprehensive research with bilingual children directly testing hypotheses regarding L2 learning processes.[1]

Naturally, the contrastive analysis theory and the L2=L1 hypothesis regarding second language learning need not be mutually exclusive. Contrastive analysis has traditionally been invoked in the context of adult second language learning, while the L2=L1 hypothesis has emerged from research with children. Underlying the L2=L1 hypothesis is the widely-held view among researchers in first-language acquisition that all languages at their most abstract level are very similar and reflect human cognitive capacities. Similarly, as was pointed out above, one version of the contrastive analysis theory makes the same assumption. Where the two theories clash is in predicting the types of errors that will be made during the learning of a second language when the first language is already known. Since children do not fully know their native language, one could expect that both developmental-type errors and contrastive-type errors would be made. With adults, of course, developmental errors would not appear during learning.

It can now be seen that Lambert and Tucker's proposal of 'incipient contrastive linguistics' as a learning process in children, a process benefitting competence in both languages, is quite novel in that it cannot neatly be placed in the two major theories of second language acquisition. It has only superficial similarity to the contrastive analysis theory, and seems outside the developmental framework of the L2=L1 hypothesis.

In summary, although many psychometric studies have been done on child bilingualism, very few studies exist which test hypotheses regarding the processes of second language learning in children. The two major theories which attempt to explain the errors made during second language learning may appear to be contradictory, but these contradictions are not inherently unresolvable, especially in the area of child language. Research on first-language acquisition has naturally influenced speculations regarding child bilingualism. In fact, some of the contradictions between current theories of bilingualism pointed out above have their counterpart, if not their origin, in the area of first-language acquisition.

Theories of first-language acquisition

Before the 1960's, researchers in the field of language development were working with a model of language which differs radically from the models currently prevailing. It was based, often implicitly, on the associationist tradition in psychology and articulated in terms of behaviorist principles. The processes of learning a language were conceived as identical to the processes of learning any other complex skill, that is, by the association of stimulus and response under reinforcement conditions. There was no fundamental difference between the way an adult learned a second language and the way a child learned his first one.

The 1960's saw a dramatic shift in the theory of language, commonly attributed to the linguistic writings of Noam Chomsky (1957, 1964). Totally new research objectives were adopted, hardly definable within the previous theoretical model. Accompanying this shift in theory was an explosion in the volume of research dealing with child language development.

Within the new theoretical framework, both linguists and psychologists argued that a child must be innately predisposed to learn his first language (Katz 1964, Chomsky 1968, McNeill 1970), and that this language learning ability decreases around the age of puberty (Lenneberg 1967). Apart from this, perhaps the most striking difference between the newer theory of language, the transformational-generative theory, and the associationist theory was its emphasis on syntax. Syntax, not the spoken word, became central both to the definition and the description of language.

The two models of language differ in many other respects, in their emphasis on which questions are meaningful to ask, in what kind of evidence is admissible, in the role of biological factors, and in the definition of learning. These differences have been described in detail by Reber (1973).

More recently a theoretical schism has been detected among researchers working under the general assumptions of the transformational-generative theory of language. Among linguists, there is disagreement on the relationship of syntax to semantics. Among psycholinguists, there is an analogous disagreement on the relationship of language to thought or, more specifically, on the relationship of language development to other cognitive abilities. This disagreement can be traced from the rationalist arguments of Chomsky and his students on the innate uniqueness of human language.

At the present time, largely due to the work of Lenneberg (1967), very little argument remains over the existence of an extensive biological basis for language. The points at issue are the specificity of the biological foundations, and, as one must naturally infer, the degree to which these biological foundations so critical to language are shared by other behaviors. . . . A Process theorist would expect to find at the core of this biological heritage a set of general information-processing mechanisms. A Content theorist would expect a specific structure that guides the development of language (Reber 1973:297).

McNeill (1970), a 'content' theorist according to Reber, argued for a Language Acquisition Device (LAD), a specific innate ability in young children to process linguistic information and actively construct the syntax of their language. The LAD, as McNeill described it, was actually a hypothetical construct which generalized the results of research in the early sixties on the acquisition of syntax in young children. This research showed that the learning of syntax could not be reduced to imitation of adult models under reinforcement conditions. Children do not just learn the words and phrases they hear. The language learning process was shown to be an active search for and experimentation with rules of construction. Children from several language groups and of approximately the same age were found to proceed in the same manner.

Recently, however, evidence has accumulated which makes the LAD hypothesis untenable in some respects. This evidence constitutes the starting point for what Reber (1973) called 'process theory' in psycholinguistics. For example, Premack's (1971) experiments with chimpanzees have challenged the idea that language, when it is defined in terms of syntax, is species-specific to humans. He found that chimpanzees can be trained to show transformational and generative skills found in the language of young children, as long as the medium for the expression of these abilities was not speech sounds.

Premack's (1971) results should not be interpreted to mean that there is nothing specifically human about natural language, but rather that the cognitive operations implicit in simple syntax are not specifically human, nor specifically linguistic. This interpretation of Premack's results is supported by studies of rule learning in children which have found that syntactic-like rules (e. g. disjunction and conditionality) are developmentally acquired and used in non-linguistic contexts (Weir 1964, King 1966, Bourne and O'Banion 1971).

Arguing from entirely different data, psycholinguists have attacked the Cartesian ideas implicit in the LAD hypothesis by showing the general cognitive bases of certain syntactic forms (Bever 1970). Slobin (1971) and Moerk (1973) pointed out various chronological correspondences between syntactic development and cognitive development in the Piagetian sense, while Bever (1971:168) stressed the need for studying language 'as an organizing communication system within which different mental and neurological mechanisms interact and modify each other. '

Language and Piagetian operations

In cognitive psychology, perhaps the most outstanding and influential theorist of this century has been Jean Piaget. Although independently arrived at, his developmental theory exhibits many of the ideas and viewpoints of 'process theory' in psycholinguistics. Parallels between Piagetian and linguistic theory have been repeatedly pointed out by researchers in both areas, but research directly relating these two aspects has been scarce.

A few studies have been done which suggest that major progress in various aspects of language development occurs during the age ranges which mark the transition from pre-operational thought to the stage of concrete operations (Hornby, Hass, and Feldman 1970, Francis 1972, Swartz and Hall 1972, Vasta and Liebert 1973), and from the stage of concrete operations to formal operations (Tremaine 1972, Paris 1973). In none of these studies, however, were the subjects tested on Piagetian tasks. The authors merely noted that large changes in linguistic performance approximately coincided with transitions between stages in Piagetian theory and research.

It should be noted that both Piaget and 'process' psycholinguists maintain that cognitive development is primary, in the sense that the cognitive level of the child will limit what sort of ideas he can express and understand in language and what sort of syntactic structures he will be able to decode and use. Nonetheless, it is not implied that the linguistic system is entirely dependent on cognition, but merely that cognition, especially in childhood, sets certain limits on language. Piaget admits that in early adolescence language can facilitate abstract reasoning.

Some researchers in North America, however, have not agreed with Piaget regarding the secondary role of language in pre-operational thought.

Perhaps the most contested part of Piaget's stage theory of development has been his proposal of an equilibration process to explain the transition between one stage and the next. Regarding the transition to the stage of concrete operations at about the age of seven or eight, Bruner (1964) proposed an alternative mechanism. 'Linguistic experience', he felt, enabled the child to free himself from the immediacy of perceptual experience and to reason correctly about the transformations of substance. In other words, he felt that conservation was induced by a certain level of language development rather than, as Piaget (1952) has suggested, by the understanding of logical operations achieved through equilibration.

Bruner (1964) cited the work of Frank, one of his students, in support of this hypothesis. Frank, using a screening device in presenting the classic conservation of liquid task, asked children to make conservation judgments without seeing the water levels. She found that screening the perceptual illusion and committing the child to a judgment before the water levels were revealed significantly increased the number of correct judgments. Bruner interpreted these findings as resulting from the suppression of lower-order perceptual responses by activating verbal responses. However, other investigators have not replicated Frank's results (Greenfield 1966, Sonstroem 1966). In fact, attempts to train children younger than five years old in conservation, either through linguistic or other means, have been notoriously unsuccessful. However, the onset of concrete operations can be accelerated by training only in the age range when children are about to discover these concepts by themselves (approximately six to eight years old), that is, when they are most susceptible to 'disequilibrium' according to Piaget and Inhelder (1969).

But perhaps the most direct test of Bruner's hypothesis was a series of studies done by Sinclair-de-Zwart (1967). Sinclair-de-Zwart studied the language of conservers and non-conservers by having them describe simple objects, often presented in pairs. Conservers used more relational terms ('more-less'), more opposites ('long-short'), and more co-ordinated descriptions of two attributes or two objects ('this pencil is longer, but that one is fatter'). Non-conservers, on the other hand, tended to describe objects one at a time, or one characteristic at a time ('this pencil is big'). The non-conservers were then subjected to intensive training in the type of language used by conservers, and were tested again on various tasks. Only minimal progress was found. About ten percent of the non-conservers advanced from one sub-state to the next. Sinclair-de-Zwart concluded that there is a close correspondence between the language used by children and their mode of reasoning, and suggested that language does not structure logic, but is, on the contrary, structured by it.

Nonetheless, the verbal method of assessing Piagetian reasoning has raised the question whether a child who misunderstands the task requirements is inaccurately judged to be a non-conserver. For example, Braine and Shanks (1965) have suggested that non-conserving children interpret 'same' to mean 'look alike' rather than numerically equivalent.

Recently, psycholinguists have become interested in this problem. Their research in semantic feature development has shown that a five-year-old's 'misunderstanding' of dimensional terms is much more systematic than that of a three-year-old (Clark 1973, Maratsos 1973). Older children's errors seem to come from their tendency to analyze increasingly along one dimension, a tendency which has been repeatedly observed among non-conservers of liquid and which Piaget called 'centring.' Maratsos (1973) pointed out that this tendency is a sign of greater semantic differentiation, that is, a sign of progress, not retardation.

Regarding the conservation of number, Rose (1973) showed that when children erred in their judgments, younger ones (three to four years old) adopted an acquiescent response set, while older ones (five to six years old) systematically confounded length and number.

It seems, therefore, that there is a close correspondence between semantic progress and systematic 'misunderstanding' of Piagetian task requirements. Young non-conservers tend to agree with the experimenter, whatever is said, while older non-conservers systematically confound height and quantity, or number and length. Although the relationship of semantic feature development to performance on Piagetian tasks needs more investigation, some tentative conclusions based on the research available can be reached regarding criticisms of Piaget's verbal methodology.

Because systematic 'misunderstanding' corresponds to a greater understanding of the adult semantic feature system, as well as to a shorter chronological distance from mastering conservation, it could be that both semantic features and conservation tasks are indices of the same developmental, cognitive process. The centring tendency of older non-conservers handicaps them in both types of experiments. This handicap, or more accurately, developmental level, can be labelled either as a 'misunderstanding of adult language' or as 'pre-operational logic'.

If this interpretation of the data is correct, then criticisms of Piaget's verbal method of gathering data from children seem entirely beside the point. In line with Sinclair-de-Zwart's (1969) view of the relationship of language to operational thought, the non-conserving child misinterprets terms such as 'same' precisely because he is not conserving.

In brief, evidence on the relationship of operational thought to language supports Piaget's (1964:5) view that '. . . language serves to translate what is already understood . . . the level of understanding seems to modify the language that is used, rather than vice versa.' But to date research supporting this view has been only suggestive. The experimental design necessary to demonstrate that language as a system depends on or is structured by operational thought was not used in any of the studies reviewed. At best, what has been demonstrated is that certain aspects of operational thought are correlated with the use of certain isolated linguistic forms, and that training in linguistic forms has little, if any, effect on some aspects of operational thought.

Linguistic theory and Piagetian operations

The major obstacle to doing developmental research relating the structure of language to the structure of operational thought has been the difficulty of defining what constitutes 'complexity' in syntax. Since development, by definition, progresses from the simple to the complex, or from the easy to the difficult, it was crucial to have some theoretical base from which syntactic structures could be sequenced in terms of complexity.

Various attempts at formalizing syntactic complexity have been reviewed elsewhere (Tremaine 1972). These attempts were unsuccessful for a variety of reasons: because too few structures were studied (Brown and Hanlon 1970), because only exceptional structures were studied (Chomsky 1969), because the rules determining complexity could not simultaneously be applied to more than one class of structures (Fodor, Garrett, and Bever 1968), or because complexity was expressed in terms that are theoretically unrevealing, e.g. number of 'less-than-predicates' (Hunt 1970).

In theoretical linguistics, a trend analogous to 'process theory' in psycholinguistics can be discerned. Within the framework of transformational grammar, various inconsistencies have been pointed out, especially those relating syntax to semantics. McCawley (1968), for example, showed how the separation of the syntactic level from the semantic level was artificial.

In tackling the vexing problems of earlier theory regarding selectional restrictions and semantic feature representation, Fillmore (1968, 1971) proposed an alternative conceptual framework, called case grammar [see Appendix A for a fuller discussion of case grammar], which collapsed the semantic-syntactic distinction. Unlike earlier theories of case in language, in Fillmore's theory, case is a deep structure notion identifying underlying syntactic-semantic relations which are realized sometimes in inflection, sometimes in prepositions or word order. Although Fillmore was primarily interested in linguistic description, his theory was particularly useful for developmental studies because it allowed an explicit definition of syntactic complexity, as well as an interrelation of numerous structures such that they could be sequenced from simple to complex.

In her study of syntactic development in English–Italian bilingual children, Kessler (1971) used Fillmore's case grammar model, together with certain modifications proposed by Di Pietro (1971). As she noted, 'almost no studies exist for child language bilingualism examined in terms of modern linguistic theory and contrastive analysis' (Kessler 1971:24). Kessler's study, although it was largely exploratory, can be viewed as a major breakthrough in linguistic and cognitive studies of children. Among other things, she found that the comprehension of an interrelated set of syntactic structures follows a maturational sequence very much like the development of operational thought. In addition, by showing that linguistic structures shared by two languages have a parallel development, she has provided a new methodology for studying the acquisition of a second language.

Summary of the Kessler (1971) study

The major aim of the study was to test the hypothesis that syntactic structures common to Italian and English develop in the same order and at the same rate in the bilingual child. In addition, the comprehension of synonymity both within and across languages was investigated.

The structures chosen to be tested were those which the literature either directly or implicitly indicated as late-developing, and which could be inter-related through case grammar and sequenced from simple to complex. Syntactic complexity was defined in terms of case relations and case expansions together with associated syntactic features. Because case grammar allows formal and explicit statements of deep structure contrasts, a comprehension test based on contrastive analysis was devised as the major tool of the study. [See Appendix A, section 1.1, for a discussion of deep and surface structure.]

Kessler also hypothesized that maturation as defined by chronological age and scores on standardized tests would be correlated with the comprehension of syntax. Certain language-specific structures were also tested if they were related to structures common to both languages. It was hypothesized that language-specific structures would be acquired after the language-shared structures to which they were related.

Selection of subjects. Subjects were selected from the six- to eight-year-old range, since in a pilot study, Kessler found that four- and five-year-old children did not comprehend the structures very well, and showed considerable restlessness and confusion. Twelve children, ten girls and two boys, were finally selected, evenly divided between Grades One and Two, based on the following criteria: (1) that the children must be bilingual, (2) that the parents must be native-born Italians, (3) that Italian must be used extensively in the home, with preference given to children who had lived in Italy or had visited there.

All subjects attended the same school, and were screened for bilingualism by both individual interviews and tests. An imitation test in two forms, one in Italian and one in English, was administered to the children, and the results taken as an indication of grammatical development in the two languages. Both forms contained grammatically well-formed sentences as well as sentences with some type of structural deviancy. The children who could repeat nearly all of the sentences, grammatical and deviant, were considered bilingual. Previous research has shown that more mature children are more likely to repeat nonsense stimuli than less mature ones (Shipley, Smith, and Gleitman 1969).

All subjects were speakers of southern Italian dialects, not the standard language, and their parents represented the same socio-economic level (same type of neighborhood, common cultural background, similar fathers' occupations). Parents and children were interviewed for their attitudes towards bilingualism, and it was found that their attitudes were very similar. All endorsed the value of bilingualism.

Test administration and design of the syntactic comprehension tests. To assess the general ability level of the children, a portion of the Stanford Early School Achievement Test (SESAT), Level 1, was administered. This section deals with auditory comprehension and correlates with the Otis-Lennon Mental Ability Test (.65).

Before testing was begun, a series of preliminary sessions was held with each child. The examiner conversed with the child and discussed pictures in

children's books in English and in Italian, during separate sessions. The
children were encouraged to retell stories heard from tape-recorded material
in both languages, and their responses were tape-recorded. To accustom the
child to the testing situation and to gain more information about his linguistic
competence, two tests of production were given--a Berko-type morphological
generalization test (Berko 1958) and a test of interrogative verb forms.

The syntactic comprehension tests were then administered individually,
after some practice items. In every case, the child showed his comprehension of the item to be tested by choosing the correct alternative within a contrasted set. The contrasts were presented either visually or aurally.

Syntactic structures and inflectional categories within languages were
tested by means of matching a tape-recorded phrase or sentence with a picture. While the child heard the tape-recorded stimulus, he was presented
with a set of three pictures on a sheet of paper. These were pictures of some
action, situation, or object which could be conveyed through a line drawing.
Two of the pictures represented the syntactic contrast to be tested, while the
third was a neutral item. The child was then required to point to that which
designated the sentence or phrase. Each structure was tested by three contrasts, or six items which were presented in random order. There were a
total of thirteen structures common to Italian and English, one Italian-
specific, and two English-specific structures, as well as six inflectional
categories.

Comprehension of synonymity both within and across languages could not,
of course, be assessed through pictures, although the same contrastive tech-
nique was used. Within languages, synonymity was assessed through syntactic variants, defined as 'the surface manifestation of an underlying deep
structure in alternate or variant modes' (e.g. relative clause/adjective contrasts). Across languages, both variants and similar structures were used.
Five structural relationships common to Italian and English formed the core
of the synonymity tests. The child heard the taped stimulus sentence, and
then two other sentences from which he was directed to choose either sentence
one or sentence two, the one 'which means the same thing as the first sentence
you hear'.

The syntactic comprehension tests were presented in what appeared to be
an increasing order of difficulty, which was: inflectional categories, syntactic structures, synonymous sentences within languages, and synonymous
sentences across languages.

Data analysis. The data were analyzed in terms of test scores (one point
for each correct response), cumulative scores for all tests in each language,
and scores for the various subparts (inflectional categories, syntactic structures, synonymity within languages, and synonymity across languages).
Correlations were determined between these scores, SESAT auditory comprehension scores, and chronological age. A factor analysis was also done.

In the light of the above results, an in-depth linguistic analysis of the
structures tested, based on the number of errors per structure, was also
done. Syntactic structures in both languages were sequenced from easy to
difficult based on errors, and this order was compared with theoretical predictions regarding complexity.

Results and their implications. The correlation matrix indicated that the comprehension tests were all measuring the same ability. This was verified by a principle component factor analysis. Based on eleven variables, factor analysis attributed 80 percent of the variance to one common factor, presumed to be language competence.

Cognitive level as measured by the SESAT auditory comprehension scores was highly correlated with levels of syntactic comprehension. Cumulative scores for both languages were highly correlated, indicating that the children had nearly achieved a balanced bilingualism or, in other words, that Kessler's time-consuming selection procedure had been successful. None of the children, however, achieved a perfect score on any of the subtests, indicating that both languages were still developing. Although correlations between language measures and chronological age were only moderate (e.g. approximately .50), it should be noted that the age range was very narrow (mean = 7.08, standard deviation = .75). However, conclusions based on the statistical portion of the analysis must remain tentative because of the small number of subjects tested.

The detailed linguistic analyses of the comprehension tests are discussed over some fifty pages of closely reasoned text. Thus, only the general outline of the results as well as the findings of particular import to the present study will be mentioned here.

Analysis of the difficulty of various structures in terms of total errors for the group produced a sequenced pattern which was approximately the same for the two languages. The sequences differed only at points where the languages were in contrast, that is, where language-specific realization rules overlay shared structures. Regarding the discussion above of contrastive-type errors as opposed to developmental errors during second language learning, it is noteworthy that Kessler's results supported both the L2 = L1 hypothesis and the linguistic version of contrastive analysis theory. That is, she found that children make the same kind of errors in both languages (developmental errors), as well as errors due to language-specific realization rules.

Kessler concluded that syntactic structures common to both languages were acquired in approximately the same order and at the same rate by bilingual children, and that the sequence was predictable from the relative complexity of the structures. Because the structures were similar between languages at the deep structure level, Kessler suggested that the languages of the bilingual child are not encoded separately, when it comes to comprehension. Language-specific realization rules may, on the other hand, be encoded separately from the common core. This conclusion was supported by the observation that, although the children spoke dialect forms of Italian (as determined from their performance in naturalistic speech), they comprehended the Standard Italian dialect of the examiner and the test stimuli with ease.

When the twelve children were divided into High and Low groups based on their cognitive level (SESAT scores), the High group consistently showed greater comprehension of the various structures. Kessler stressed, however, that the sequential pattern observed for the group did not necessarily hold for each individual. She interpreted this finding in terms of 'rule stabilization'. Because language acquisition was viewed as a rule-based process, 'acquisition of specific structures rests on stabilization of the rules governing that structure. As a result of rule instability, children fluctuate in the application of a rule. This necessarily gives unique results for each child. Rule acquisitions may, however, be defined for a group' (97-98).

This notion of rule instability as a learning principle is very reminiscent of Piaget's discussions of the equilibration process. The sequential order of mastering conservation on various tasks also can only be defined for the group, not for any one child. Piaget (1971) used the concept of equilibration to explain the sequential character of cognitive development, the fact that intelligence evolves through a series of stages in constant order. Each stage is defined by the achievement of a relatively stable equilibrium in the organization of mental structures, and each successive stage defines greater stability over the previous one. The impetus for moving from one stage to the next comes from experience which can only partially be assimilated by the present organization of concepts. Attempts to change the child's mode of thought, therefore, should be more successful when he is exposed to concepts that reflect a slightly higher rather than a lower stage of development. This prediction has recently been confirmed (Silverman and Geiringer 1973).

Rule stabilization and equilibration could be taken as explanatory principles referring to the same kind of learning processes. The analyses of auditory comprehension of syntactic variants both within and across languages also supports this analogy between operational thought and syntactic development. The children of Kessler's sample found this task exceptionally difficult, especially when it was presented across languages. The sequencing of these structures revealed a learning plateau, where a whole series of structures appeared to be equally undifferentiated. Kessler theorized that such a plateau pattern supported Piaget's theory, in that certain cognitive capacities necessary to comprehend syntactic variants were not yet developed in the age group of children tested.

In her suggestions for further research, Kessler stressed, among other things, the need for studies which correlate language acquisition tasks with Piagetian-type tasks, for replication of her type of analysis using different languages, and for studies where the child's second language is considerably less well developed than the first.

Recapitulation of the issues

The recent revolution in thought about the nature of language has created a curious dilemma for theories of language learning. On the one hand, strictly empiricist explanations of language learning are now considered inadequate, while nativistic explanations of the same ability are being discredited. An emergent 'process' theory has sought to avoid both extremes by considering language as only one manifestation of more general cognitive abilities. Yet this new theoretical position is still faced with the problem of explaining how language is 'learned', if it is not learned by the traditionally accepted learning principles in psychology.

In the realm of cognitive development, Piaget has faced this dilemma by positing an equilibration process to explain the sequential, cumulative acquisition of logical operations. Although Piaget's theory has been repeatedly confirmed regarding the stages through which children pass, equilibration as a general learning principle was neglected by researchers until very recently because of the difficulty of translating such an idea into an experimental design. Silverman and Geiringer's (1973) ingenious experiment supporting equilibration broke new ground. It seemed possible that a learning process such as equilibration could be operating in children's learning of language.

Research suggesting that certain aspects of language and aspects of operational intelligence were closely related was therefore discussed. Especially relevant in this respect is Sinclair-de-Zwart's (1967) research which showed that the language used by operational children is qualitatively different from the language of pre-operational children. Similarly, it was argued that semantic feature development revealed itself in the characteristic 'centring' judgments of pre-operational children. It seemed highly likely that intelligence as measured by Piagetian tasks was an ability which also showed itself in the comprehension of syntax, and that 'rule stabilization' and equilibration were explanatory principles of the same developmental phenomenon. The results of Kessler's (1971) study constantly suggested such a possibility.

Problems investigated in this study

It was therefore decided to use Piagetian measures of intelligence together with Kessler-type syntactic comprehension measures to gain further insight into the relationship of language and thought during development, and into the processes of language learning during childhood. By using English-speaking children who were learning French through a school curriculum, it was also possible to partially replicate Kessler's study of Italian-English bilinguals (1971) with French-English bilinguals, and to test Lambert and Tucker's (1972) hypothesis regarding 'incipient contrastive linguistics'.

Since children begin to master the simplest conservation tasks around the age of seven or eight, the age range of Kessler's subjects (six to eight) was both too narrow and the average age was too low to observe the major transition to the stage of concrete operations. In the present study, it was decided to use subjects between the ages of six and ten, that is, in Grades One, Two, and Three.

The major problem investigated in this study was the relationship of operational level to syntactic comprehension in children who were learning French as their second language through a school curriculum, beginning in Grade One. It was predicted that when children are able to show operational reasoning defining the stage of concrete operations, their comprehension of syntax in both languages would improve greatly. This prediction was based on the notion that 'rule stabilization' in syntax may be the same kind of process as equilibration in Piagetian theory. No predictions could be made regarding which sort of Piagetian tasks and which sort of linguistic structures would be related in this manner, although this question, too, was investigated.

It was possible to test the hypothesis that increased exposure to a second language facilitates the continued learning of the first one. Lambert and Tucker (1972) discussed this idea in terms of contrasting vocabulary items and inferring rule differences between languages, such as rules regarding word order. Therefore, it was predicted that the more a child is exposed to French, the better will be his syntactic comprehension of English. Amount of exposure to French was defined in terms of two factors: the amount of daily instruction in the French language, and the number of years the children were exposed to French at school. It was possible that some minimum amount of exposure to French was necessary before the facilitative effects on English could be manifested.

Another aim of the study was to see whether 'balanced' English-French bilingual children comprehend syntactic structures common to both languages in the same manner as described in Kessler's study with English-Italian bilinguals. However, the performance of only a subgroup of children used in the present study was applicable to this question (e.g. children in Grades One and Two, with a mean age of seven and a standard deviation of approximately .75 years, whose cumulative scores on syntactic comprehension tests of both languages were highly correlated). Nonetheless, the manner of learning the second language differed greatly between the children who formed Kessler's sample and the children used in this study. That is, Kessler's subjects learned Italian from their parents beginning in their earliest childhood, while the subjects of this study learned French at school beginning at about the age of six. No specific predictions, therefore, could be made regarding a comparison of these subjects, but it was felt that such a comparison would be revealing regarding the effects of different learning contexts on syntactic comprehension of a second language.

Another question investigated was whether the continued learning of both English and French, with French being the weaker language, would still follow the pattern described by Kessler for balanced bilinguals. If syntactic development could be described in this manner for children who were not equally competent in both languages, more generality could be attributed to the findings of Kessler's study.

NOTE

1. The notable exception is, of course, Kessler's (1971) study on the acquisition of syntax in Italian-English bilingual children which strongly supported the L2 = L1 hypothesis. Kessler's study is basic to the present study and will be discussed in considerable detail in later sections.

CHAPTER TWO

RESEARCH METHOD

The subject sample. The subjects who formed the sample were primary school children at St. Andrew's School, Ottawa, a school of the Ottawa Roman Catholic Separate School Board, which offers either of two programs for their primary school children, French immersion or 75 minutes of French per day. In Grades One and Two of the French immersion program, all subjects are taught in French (mathematics, social studies, art, physical education, language arts, and science) by a French-speaking teacher, except religious studies which are taught by an English-speaking teacher. In Grade Three, French immersion, 75 minutes per day of English language arts was introduced because it was found that the French immersion children began to lag behind other children in their English reading and spelling skills. All other subjects, except religious studies, are also taught in French in Grade Three, French immersion. The other program option consists of 75 minutes of instruction in French language arts per day, taught by a French-speaking teacher, while all other subjects are taught in English. This program will be referred to as the 75-minute program.

Parents have the option of choosing which of the two programs, French immersion or 75-minute, their child will attend, although school officials may suggest that a child be withdrawn from French immersion because of 'inability to cope' with intensive training in a second language. As a result, the French immersion group may differ from the 75-minute group in more ways than amount of exposure to the French language. A selection procedure in favor of the immersion group may be operating in increasingly higher grades since children who 'cannot cope' with French for whatever reason tend to be dropped from the program, while the children who remain in the program can be expected to be more motivated to learn French, since their parents obviously value the acquisition of this skill.

Five boys and five girls were randomly selected from each of Grades One, Two, and Three, French immersion and 75-minute classes near the end of the school year. The total number of subjects was sixty.

Children in whose homes a language other than English was habitually spoken (e.g. Italian, Polish, Ukranian) were excluded from the pool from which the random selection was made. However, children whose school records showed that they have had some contact with the French language at home (i.e. their father was taking a course in order to learn French, their aunt spoke French, etc.) were included as possible subjects, because otherwise there would not have been enough children to make a random selection. Although it would have been preferable to have subjects with no previous contact with the French language, this was next to impossible in the Ottawa area. In any case, almost all of the children had some exposure to French in kindergarten.

The mean ages and standard deviations for the three grades, expressed in years with months converted to decimals, were as follows: Grade One, mean = 6. 89, s. d. = . 31; Grade Two, mean = 7. 93, s. d. = . 22; Grade Three, mean = 9. 09, s. d. = . 29. The youngest subjects were about 6. 5 years while the oldest were about 10. 0 years. The mean age for all of the subjects was 7. 97 years, standard deviation . 97.

The Piagetian tests

Two realms of concrete operational thought were tested, conservation concepts and numeration concepts. The tasks were chosen so that they would vary in difficulty, but that all would be within the grasp of at least some of the oldest subjects. The test series consisted of five tasks--seriation, numeration, conservation of mass, conservation of weight, and conservation of volume.

The tests and materials

Seriation and numeration. Piaget (1941) formulated the seriation and numeration experiments from which these tasks were adapted in order to explore how children understood the relations between ordination and cardination in the development of number concepts. Elkind (1964) replicated Piaget's experiments and described in detail a method of questioning children on these concepts. Elkind's methodology was used in this study.

The seriation task required the child to seriate a set of ten slats (flat, rectangular pieces of painted wood) from the shortest to the longest, to form a 'staircase'. When this was done, the child was given nine more slats and told to put them in their correct place among the slats already seriated to form a longer series. In order to do this task correctly, the child had to coordinate transitive relations, such that each slat Y was represented as both larger and smaller than an adjacent slat (X<Y<Z).[1]

Each slat was 1/4-inch thick and 1-3/4-inch wide. The first set of ten slats differed in length by 1/2-inch, the shortest being 1-3/4-inch. The second set of nine slats also differed in length by 1/2-inch, but the shortest was 2-inches. The complete set of nineteen slats, therefore, differed by 1/4-inch and ranged from 1-3/4-inch to 6-1/4-inch. Each slat had a Greek letter painted on it so that the tester could record exactly how the child seriated the slats.

For the numeration task, the first set of ten slats was placed in seriated order before the child, a small plastic figure of a man ('the farmer') was produced, and the child was questioned about how many stairs the farmer had to climb to reach a particular slat. The staircase was then broken up so that the slats were disarranged, and the same types of questions were asked. The child was also asked how many stairs the farmer would have to climb to reach the top of the staircase, if he was already standing somewhere on the staircase. Before replying, the child had to reconstruct part of the series either visually or manually. The numeration task tested the child's ability to attribute cardinal value to an ordinal series, and to manipulate the series as a set of classes.

Conservation of mass and weight. The notion of conservation, or invariance of certain attributes of matter, is basic to human cognition and essential to any kind of measurement. A quantity such as a lump of plasticene, a collection of beads, a length, or a volume can be manipulated as a unit by the mind only if it remains permanent in amount and independent of the rearrangement of its parts.

The conservation of mass and weight were tested using lumps of Play-Doh. The child was presented with four Play-Doh balls of different colors, two of which were the same size while the other two were larger or smaller. The child was asked to choose the two which had the same amount of Play-Doh, or the two which weighed the same.

For both the conservation of mass and weight tasks, the shape of one of the balls was variously transformed, and the child was questioned about the equivalence of the two lumps of Play-Doh, and the reasons for his judgments. The questioning method was adapted from Elkind (1961) and Rothenberg (1969).

Conservation of solid volume. The questioning procedure for this task was adapted from Brainerd (1971). A one-pint clear plastic beaker about two-thirds full of water with an elastic band around it was shown to the child. A plasticene ball was then placed in the beaker and the child marked the water level with the elastic band. The ball was then removed from the water, its shape variously transformed, and the child answered a series of questions about what would happen to the water level if the plasticene was placed in the water.

Testing procedure

The tests were administered over a period of two weeks in May and June, 1973.

The number of subjects per group was too small to allow a complete counterbalancing of the order of test presentation. Therefore, the tests were arranged from easiest to most difficult (within the two major concept areas of numeration and conservation), and the order of administration was the same for all subjects--that is, seriation, numeration, conservation of mass, conservation of weight, and conservation of volume. Any practice effects resulting from the fixed order should have worked against finding differences between the grades, and therefore against some hypotheses of this study.

The Grade One children were tested by two female examiners, one of whom, together with a third female examiner, tested the Grade Two and Grade Three children.

The classes from which the subjects were drawn were shown a short, entertaining film by the examiners and were later asked to draw a picture from the film they saw, while the examiners supervised the class. In this way, the examiners hoped to become familiar to the children and associated with entertaining activities. The children were then told that some of them would be given tests over the next couple of weeks. Since the children at St. Andrew's School were part of a large assessment program of the Ottawa

Roman Catholic Separate School Board, they were quite familiar with testers coming to the school and taking children from class individually, so that this announcement was taken as routine.

Two children at a time were taken from their class and tested individually. Each subject was led to a testing area where he sat at a table across from the examiner. Due to limited space facilities at the school, the testing areas were far from ideal, since they faced large windows looking onto the street. Nonetheless, the Piagetian tasks seemed to interest the children considerably, so that their attention was seldom distracted. The tests took about 30 to 40 minutes per child to administer.

The time of day when the children were tested could not be controlled between grades and between the two types of curricula since teachers expressed certain time preferences when they could excuse subjects from class activities.

Method of scoring

Two different methods of scoring the Piagetian test results were used. In the first method (Method 1, Appendix B), one point was assigned for correct solutions at each step in a particular task, and the total score for the task was the sum of these points. This numerical method is widely used by Piagetian researchers because it allows a differentiation of various levels within the transition stage. Method 1 was used in this study to obtain scores which were used for supplementary analyses only, such as correlations.

The major hypotheses of the study were tested with the results of the second method of scoring (Method 2, Appendix B). The second method consisted of assigning each subject on each task to one of two nominal groups, operational or non-operational, according to Piaget's classical criteria. This method is more stringent in determining whether a child's reasoning exhibits operational structures because performance on a task as a whole is evaluated. The second method is also more theoretically sound because the difference between pre-operational and operational thought is a qualitative difference which does not lend itself to quantification. This is especially true because the stage of transition is still a poorly understood process.

Because Method 2 required some degree of subjective judgment on the part of the scorer, the independent judgments of two scorers (the experimenter and a doctoral student in developmental psychology) were compared for a sample of the subjects' test protocols to obtain an indication of the reliability of this method of scoring. The protocols of twenty subjects (one-third of the sample) were scored in this fashion. These protocols required 100 independent judgments regarding the operational level of the subjects. There was 99 percent agreement between the judges.

The syntactic comprehension tests

The tests and materials. Kessler's original syntactic contrasts in English and Italian were obtained and a test was constructed for English–French syntactic comprehension. A subset of Kessler's structures were selected for testing, with a few lexical changes. Appendix C lists the contrasts tested in the study together with their description in terms of case grammar and syntactic features. A full description of these structures, their interrelation, and relative complexity, may be found in Kessler (1971). In a personal communication, Kessler noted that some of her pictures could be improved upon since they may have presented ambiguities. A complete set of line drawings original to this investigation was therefore prepared (Appendix D).

Each syntactic structure was tested by two contrasts, or four items, unlike the procedure used by Kessler which tested each structure by three contrasts, or six items. This shortening of the test was felt to be necessary since in a pilot study it was found that the younger children became restless and distractable after about 30 minutes of testing. (The longer version of the test took about 45 minutes.)

The syntactic comprehension tests were divided into three major parts: an English test, a French test, and an across-languages test.

The English and French tests were each divided into three sections which were administered in the consecutive order below:

(1) Six inflectional categories shared by the two languages were tested by fourteen contrasts, or twenty-eight items (a picture test).
(2) Eleven syntactic structures shared by the two languages were tested by twenty-two contrasts, or forty-four items (a picture test).
(3) Five syntactic variants within languages were tested by five contrasts, or ten items (an auditory test).

Within each section, the items were randomly ordered and presented in the same order to all subjects. [A listing of the inflectional and syntactic structures and syntactic variants appears in Appendix C, pp. 70-79. Appendix C provides examples of the syntactic contrasts tested in this study.]

The across-languages test, an auditory test, was divided into two sections:

(1) Four similar syntactic structures across languages were tested by means of eight items, four of which tested comprehension from French to English, while the other four tested comprehension from English to French. The four English-to-French items were presented first, then the four French-to-English.
(2) Six syntactic variants were tested across languages by means of twelve items, six of which tested comprehension from French to English, while the other six tested comprehension from English to French. The six French-to-English items were presented first.

The items in each section of the across-languages test were not randomized, but presented in blocks according to the language of the stimulus sentence because of certain observations made during a pilot study. It was found that this test was quite difficult for some children, in that it required their undivided attention. When items switched between English-to-French and French-to-English as they did when randomly ordered, the children seemed confused and their interest and attention rapidly declined. On the other hand, when the test items were grouped as described above, children seemed quite at ease with the test. Appendix E lists the actual order in which the items were presented for the English, French, and across-language tests.

Testing procedure. All subjects were given the full set of syntactic comprehension tests during a three-week period in May, 1973. An

English-speaking female examiner administered the English test, while another fluently bilingual female examiner administered the French test and, immediately after, the across-languages test. Half of the children in each sub-group were tested in English first, while the other half were tested in French first. That is, five children in Grades One, Two, and Three, immersion, and 75-minute classes, were administered the French test series first. An interval of at least one day separated the French test series from the English test series for each child.

The children were tested individually in the testing area provided by St. Andrew's School. The English test series took about 25 minutes to administer, while the French test series took about 15 minutes longer due to the across-languages test. The French examiner took a short break between the French test and the across-languages test to chat with the subject in French and give him a piece of candy.

Kessler's testing procedure was modified in two major ways. First, the stimulus sentences or phrases were not tape-recorded, but read by the examiner at a rate which suited each individual child. In a pilot study it was found that children varied considerably in their rate of responding to the pictures, regardless of their knowledge of the language in question. When the stimuli were tape-recorded, the intervals of silence between items found some children awkwardly waiting for the next item, while other children would be still in the process of making up their minds while scanning the pictures. The procedure of reading the stimulus phrase while presenting the set of three pictures was therefore adopted, and the next item was not read until the child had ample time to make his choice.

The second major procedural modification was in the presentation of the tests for comprehension of synonymous sentences. In the pilot study, the sentences were tape-recorded and the child was directed to say 'Sentence 1' or 'Sentence 2' indicating his choice, as was done in Kessler's study. This procedure was judged to be inadequate because the children for whom this test was difficult tended to answer randomly and not pay attention. The procedure adopted in the study, therefore, was to read the stimulus sentence and then, after a short pause, the two sentences from which the child made his choice, while maintaining the child's attention by eye-contact and an enthusiastic attitude, as if this was an extremely clever riddle that the child could solve if he tried. This sort of attitude on the part of the examiner proved to be most successful in keeping the attention and interest of the subjects. After the test series, several children commented that the part they enjoyed most was the one where 'you asked me what things mean the same'. The child had to make his choice between the two alternatives by verbalizing as much of the chosen sentence as he could, instead of a non-committal 'Sentence 1' or 'Sentence 2'. In this way, it was possible to be sure that the child at least listened to the sentence he chose.

Before the actual test items were presented, the subjects were given some practice items to familiarize them with the procedure. In the case of the French picture tests, these practice items were also intended to drill subjects in vocabulary items which they may not know. The pilot study indicated that even the Grade One, 75-minute subjects were familiar with most of the French words used in the tests. Those few words which were at times unfamiliar were subsequently drilled in the practice items (la souris, l'avion, le pilote, le château, le roi, le camion, la voiture).

For the practice items before the picture tests, the examiner said, in either French or English: 'We're going to play a game with pictures. First I will say a word or sentence. You point to the picture which means what I say. Here are three pictures. Show me the boy. Show me the boy with the dog. . . . Show me the boy running. . . They are running . . . etc.'

For auditory comprehension of synonymous sentences within languages, the examiner said: 'I will say a sentence. Listen to this sentence carefully and try to remember. Then I will say two other sentences. You tell me which of the two sentences mean the same as the first sentence.' These instructions were usually understood by the subjects only after several practice items. For practice, the examiner then said: 'Now listen. The boy sees a dog and a cat. Does that mean the same as (pause) the boy sees the cat, or (slight pause), the boy sees the cat and the dog?' Similar practice items were given until it was clear that the child understood what was required, and until he knew that he had to verbalize his choice as well as he could. A similar procedure was used for the across-languages test, except that the examiner said in English: 'Now I will say a sentence in English, and then two sentences in French . . . etc.' When it came time for the French-to-English items, no further instructions were required, since all of the children fell naturally into the procedure.

Method of scoring. The examiner checked off on an answer sheet the picture that the subject pointed to or the sentence which he repeated. (For a sample of the answer sheet, see Appendix E.) The answer sheets were then scored by awarding the subject one point for the correct choice on each item, and totaling the correct items for each syntactic structure or inflectional category.

Design and hypotheses

The questions which this study hoped to answer, formulated in the previous chapter, can be summarized as follows:

(A) How is operational level related to syntactic comprehension of French and English?

(B) Does increased exposure to French facilitate the syntactic comprehension of English?

(C) Do 'balanced' English-French bilingual children comprehend syntactic structures common to both languages in the same manner as described in Kessler's study?

(D) When one language is weaker than the other, does the continued learning of both languages still follow the pattern described by Kessler for 'balanced' bilingual children? That is, are the theoretically more complex structures of the weaker language acquired later than the theoretically simpler structures?

The dependent variable for each of the above questions was performance on the syntactic comprehension tests. Questions A and B required statistical analyses, while questions C and D were exploratory and intended to replicate Kessler's findings with different languages and older subjects. Kessler's analytic method was therefore used to answer questions C and D. That is, the number of errors per syntactic structure was determined for both types of curricula at each grade level. The structures were then sequenced in order of difficulty, and the sequences were compared between French and English, and between Kessler's findings with English and Italian and the present findings with English and French.

In order to answer questions A and B, performance on the syntactic comprehension tests was defined in terms of the number of correct items in the following linguistic categories (see Appendix C):

(1) English inflectional categories
(2) English syntactic structures
(3) English synonymous sentences within languages
(4) Cumulative English score (total of 1, 2, and 3)
(5) French inflectional categories
(6) French syntactic structures
(7) French synonymous sentences within languages
(8) Cumulative French score (total of 5, 6, and 7)
(9) Synonymous sentences across languages, similar structures
(10) Synonymous sentences across languages, syntactic variants
(11) Cumulative across-languages score (total of 9 and 10)

The independent variables relevant to questions A and B were as follows:

(1) Operational level on each of the five Piagetian tasks (two levels: non-operational and operational)
(2) The amount of exposure to French as defined by an intensity factor (two levels: 75-minute curriculum and Immersion curriculum)
(3) The amount of exposure to French as defined by a time factor (three levels: Grades One, Two, and Three).

The hypotheses tested by means of statistical analyses (questions A and B) can now be stated in terms of the above variables:

Hypothesis 1. Performance on the English, French, and across-languages tests will be significantly better by children classified as operational than by children classified as non-operational on each of the five Piagetian tasks.

Hypothesis 2. Performance on the English test will be significantly better by children in the immersion curriculum than by children in the 75-minute curriculum.

Hypothesis 3. Performance on the English test will be significantly better by children in increasingly higher grades.

Hypothesis 4. The time and intensity factors of the amount of exposure to French (i. e. grade and curriculum) will interact significantly in performance on the English test.

The rationale for Hypothesis 4 was based on the possibility that some minimum amount of exposure to French would be necessary before the facilitative effects on English could be manifested.

Statistical analyses

Hypothesis 1 was tested by means of one-way multivariate and univariate analyses of variance for the operational factor (two levels) for each of the five

Piagetian tasks. Hypotheses 2, 3, and 4 were tested by means of two-way multivariate and univariate analyses of variance for the curriculum (two levels) and grade (three levels) factors. One-way analyses of covariance were also done for each of the three factors, using the other two factors as covariates.

A Pearson product moment intercorrelation matrix of all the variables used in the study was obtained. Excluding the three dependent variables which represented cumulative scores (e.g. dependent variables 4, 8, and 11), a principal components/principal axis factor analysis with varimax rotation was done using all of the variables in the study.

NOTE

1. For a detailed description of the questioning and scoring procedure for all of the Piagetian tests, see Appendix B.

CHAPTER THREE

RESULTS

Statistical analyses. Initial analyses of variance for the sex, grade, and curriculum factors showed no significant differences on any of the eleven syntactic measures or chronological age for the main effect of sex, or the interaction of sex with either or both of the other two factors.[1] In most subsequent analyses, the sex factor was therefore not analyzed.

Chronological age was highly significant for the main effect of grade ($F = 189.58$; df $= 2/48$; $p < .001$) but not significant for curriculum. Scheffé post hoc contrasts between the means for chronological age of each two grades were significant at less than the .05 level. The interaction of grade and curriculum was not significant for chronological age.

Table 1 shows the means and standard deviations of the scores obtained by the total sample on the eleven syntactic subtests.[2] (See above for a definition of the subtests and Appendix C for a list of the contrasts tested in each subtest.) The intercorrelations of all the variables in the study are shown in Table 2.

TABLE 1. Means and standard deviations of scores obtained by the total sample on the eleven syntactic subtests

Subtest	No. of items per subtest	Mean score	s. d.
1. EI	28	22.83	1.38
2. ESS	44	36.95	4.16
3. ESY	10	8.38	1.92
4. FI	28	20.85	4.25
5. FSS	44	34.45	5.98
6. FSY	10	7.25	2.25
7. A-S	8	6.42	1.38
8. A-V	12	9.17	2.34
9. CE	82	70.17	6.65
10. CF	82	62.55	11.50
11. CA	20	15.58	3.41

Many of the variables are highly correlated, especially the two methods of scoring the Piagetian tests. In view of the fact that an $r = .35$ is significant

24

TABLE 2. Intercorrelation matrix of twenty-five variables

Variables*	1	2	3	4	5	6	7	8	9	10	11	12	13	14	15	16	17	18	19	20	21	22	23	24	25
1	1.00																								
2	.00	1.00																							
3	.00	.00	1.00																						
4	.09	.30	.29	1.00																					
5	-.06	.57	.20	.39	1.00																				
6	.10	.54	.10	.40	.58	1.00																			
7	.17	.25	.17	.31	.38	.48	1.00																		
8	-.06	.30	-.06	.12	.30	.24	.38	1.00																	
9	-.08	.93	-.06	.25	.54	.51	.25	.27	1.00																
10	.00	.48	.24	.38	.41	.48	.27	.26	.44	1.00															
11	.02	.74	.24	.33	.65	.66	.41	.34	.63	.62	1.00														
12	.04	.70	.13	.49	.59	.59	.25	.26	.65	.57	.70	1.00													
13	.03	.76	.24	.43	.66	.68	.39	.34	.67	.76	.96	.85	1.00												
14	.02	.50	.59	.50	.71	.52	.40	.31	.44	.47	.66	.70	.71	1.00											
15	.06	.60	.49	.55	.62	.54	.41	.31	.53	.62	.74	.64	.78	.81	1.00										
16	-.07	.50	.43	.37	.57	.41	.36	.26	.46	.26	.51	.58	.54	.74	.69	1.00									
17	.02	.60	.56	.54	.69	.55	.43	.33	.53	.55	.73	.71	.77	.93	.95	.82	1.00								
18	-.04	.31	.47	.16	.52	.42	.41	.22	.29	.30	.52	.37	.50	.71	.58	.52	.67	1.00							
19	.03	.61	.42	.37	.57	.45	.40	.26	.54	.35	.62	.60	.63	.77	.72	.77	.81	.65	1.00						
20	.01	.54	.48	.31	.61	.48	.44	.27	.49	.36	.64	.56	.64	.82	.73	.74	.83	.85	.95	1.00					
21	.08	.32	.30	.38	.38	.40	.30	.11	.27	.45	.33	.52	.45	.51	.59	.38	.57	.18	.36	.33	1.00				
22	-.03	.49	.27	.62	.87	.62	.42	.26	.48	.55	.62	.66	.69	.72	.71	.61	.76	.52	.54	.58	.66	1.00			
23	.05	.42	.19	.52	.60	.48	.21	.42	.51	.56	.57	.62	.53	.62	.44	.61	.36	.45	.45	.53	.69	.49	1.00		
24	-.08	.14	.22	.39	.43	.45	.34	.14	.34	.27	.36	.30	.37	.53	.40	.34	.44	.40	.35	.40	.38	.49	.55	1.00	
25	.01	.43	.05	.21	.39	.43	.39	.49	.86	.36	.30	.45	.38	.46	.45	.41	.37	.45	.30	.39	.39	.20	.39	.35	.46	1.00

*Variables

1 Sex
2 Grade
3 Curriculum
4 Ser. level
5 Num. level

6 Mass level
7 Weight level
8 Volume level
9 Age
10 EI

11 ESS
12 ESY
13 CE
14 FI
15 FSS

16 FSY
17 CF
18 A-S
19 A-V
20 CA

21 Ser. score
22 Num. score
23 Mass score
24 Weight score
25 Volume score

at the .01 level, operational level was highly correlated with the syntactic measures, especially for the numeration, conservation of mass, and conservation of weight tasks.

Operational level differences. Table 3 shows the number of subjects who were classified as non-operational and operational on the five Piagetian tasks by curriculum and grade. The small number of subjects in many cells did not allow a simultaneous analysis of variance for the three factors of curriculum, grade, and operational level.

TABLE 3. Number of subjects classified as non-operational and operational for the five Piagetian tasks by curriculum and grade

	Seriation		Numeration		Mass		Weight		Volume	
	nonop	op	nonop	op	nonop	op	nonop	op	nonop	op
75-minute Curriculum										
Grade 1	5	5	8	2	8	2	8	2	10	0
Grade 2	1	9	7	3	2	8	7	3	9	1
Grade 3	1	9	3	7	3	7	6	4	8	2
Total	7	23	18	12	13	17	21	9	27	3
Immersion Curriculum										
Grade 1	1	9	9	1	8	2	7	3	10	0
Grade 2	0	10	3	7	2	8	6	4	10	0
Grade 3	0	10	0	10	0	10	3	7	8	2
Total	1	29	12	18	10	20	16	14	28	2

As expected from previous studies, it is evident from Table 3 that the seriation task was the easiest and the conservation of volume task the most difficult for this subject sample. Most of the subjects could seriate, while very few could conserve volume.

Table 4 presents the multivariate and univariate F-ratios for the analysis of variance of eight syntactic subtest scores and three syntactic cumulative scores for the operational factor (seriation, numeration, conservation of mass, conservation of weight, and conservation of volume). The univariate analyses for all five Piagetian tasks were significant at less than the .05 level for all the syntactic subtests, except for seriation and conservation of volume on the across-languages (similar structures) subtest. The multivariate analyses for all Piagetian tasks were also significant at less than the .05 level, except for the conservation of volume on the eight syntactic subtests. Therefore, out of 65 independent analyses of variance testing Hypothesis 1, 62 of them confirmed the prediction that children classified as operational will perform significantly better on syntactic comprehension tests in English, French, and across languages.

Exposure to French differences. Table 5 presents the multivariate and univariate F-ratios for the analysis of variance of three English subtest scores for the intensity (curriculum) and time (grade) factors of the amount of exposure to French. The main effects of curriculum and grade were significant at less than the .05 level for the multivariate and univariate

TABLE 4. Multivariate and univariate F-ratios for the analysis of variance of eight syntactic subtest scores and three syntactic cumulative scores for the Operational factor

	SERIATION				NUMERATION			
	Multivariate ANOVA		Univariate ANOVA		Multivariate ANOVA		Univariate ANOVA	
	df	F	df	F	df	F	df	F
Subtest	8/51	4.97**			8/51	8.47**		
1. EI			1/58	9.92**			1/58	11.99**
2. ESS			1/58	6.98*			1/58	42.40**
3. ESY			1/58	18.35**			1/58	30.27**
4. FI			1/58	19.12**			1/58	58.25**
5. FSS			1/58	25.29**			1/58	35.46**
6. FSY			1/58	9.39**			1/58	28.59**
7. A-S			1/58	1.43			1/58	21.86**
8. A-V			1/58	8.94**			1/58	28.42**
Cumulative Subtest	3/56	10.18**			3/56	20.53**		
1. CE			1/58	12.86**			1/58	45.19**
2. CF			1/58	24.30**			1/58	53.93**
3. CA			1/58	6.36*			1/58	33.66**
n(non-operational) = 8					n(non-operational) = 30			
n(operational) = 52					n(operational) = 30			
	CONSERVATION OF MASS				CONSERVATION OF WEIGHT			
	Multivariate ANOVA		Univariate ANOVA		Multivariate ANOVA		Univariate ANOVA	
	df	F	df	F	df	F	df	F
Subtest	8/51	5.94**			8/51	2.14*		
1. EI			1/58	17.37**			1/58	4.61*
2. ESS			1/58	45.47**			1/58	11.59**
3. ESY			1/58	30.96**			1/58	4.03*
4. FI			1/58	21.15**			1/58	11.19**
5. FSS			1/58	23.88**			1/58	12.03**
6. FSY			1/58	11.76**			1/58	8.46**
7. A-S			1/58	12.07**			1/58	11.76**
8. A-V			1/58	15.11**			1/58	11.08**
Cumulative Subtest	3/56	16.72**			3/56	5.15**		
1. CE			1/58	51.24**			1/58	10.11**
2. CF			1/58	21.41**			1/58	13.45**
3. CA			1/58	17.41**			1/58	14.05**
n(non-operational) = 23					n(non-operational) = 37			
n(operational) = 37					n(operational) = 23			
	CONSERVATION OF VOLUME							
	Multivariate ANOVA		Univariate ANOVA					
	df	F	df	F				
Subtest	8/51	1.02						
1. EI			1/58	4.10*				
2. ESS			1/58	7.56**				
3. ESY			1/58	4.05*				
4. FI			1/58	6.22*				
5. FSS			1/58	6.30*				
6. FSY			1/58	4.32*				
7. A-S			1/58	2.85				
8. A-V			1/58	4.33*				
Cumulative Subtest	3/56	2.80*						
1. CE			1/58	7.56**				
2. CF			1/58	7.05**				
3. CA			1/58	4.52*				
n(non-operational) = 55								
n(operational) = 5								

*p < .05
**p < .01

TABLE 5. Multivariate and univariate F-ratios for the analysis of variance
of three English subtest scores for the curriculum and grade
factors

Source of variance	Multivariate ANOVA		Univariate ANOVA	
	df	F	df	F
Curriculum (C)	3/52	2.93*		
1. EI			1/54	4.76*
2. ESS			1/54	7.82**
3. ESY			1/54	2.31
Grade (G)	6/104	14.85**		
1. EI			2/54	9.43**
2. ESS			2/54	37.51**
3. ESY			2/54	38.77**
Interaction (C X G)	6/104	1.09		
1. EI			2/54	1.30
2. ESS			2/54	.49
3. ESY			2/54	.40

*$p < .05$
**$p < .01$

analyses, except for the curriculum factor on English synonymous sentences.
The interaction of curriculum and grade was not significant for any of the analyses. The immersion children, therefore, performed significantly better than
the 75-minute children on tests of English inflectional categories and English
syntactic structures, but there was no significant difference between the curricula on English synonymous sentences.

Table 6 presents the significance levels for contrasts between group means
for the grade factor. For the univariate analyses, Scheffé post hoc contrasts
were calculated, showing that children in increasingly higher grades performed significantly better in every case, except between Grades Two and
Three on English inflectional categories and English synonymous sentences.
For the multivariate analysis, post hoc contrasts using θ's (the multivariate
analog to Scheffé contrasts) showed the same pattern, except that English
inflectional categories did not statistically differentiate any two grades.

TABLE 6. Significance levels for contrasts between group means from
the multivariate and univariate analyses of variance of three
English subtest scores for the grade factor

	Contrast between grades		
	1, 3	2, 3	1, 2
Multivariate ANOVA			
1. EI	ns	ns	ns
2. ESS	**	**	**
3. ESY	**	ns	**
Univariate ANOVA			
1. EI	**	ns	*
2. ESS	**	**	**
3. ESY	**	ns	**

*$p < .05$
**$p < .01$

Analyses of covariance

The operational factor. In view of the above results which showed that all three independent variables (operational level, curriculum, grade) were to a greater or lesser extent significant for performance on the syntactic comprehension tests, it was possible that operational level was significant because children in increasingly higher grades tended to be classified as operational more often (see Table 3). Similarly, children in the immersion curriculum tended to be classified as operational more often than children in the 75-minute curriculum. It was not possible to decide from the above analyses whether operational level would be significant for the five Piagetian tasks when the effects of grade and curriculum were removed.

A one-way analysis of covariance using operational level on each Piagetian task as the independent variable and the curriculum and grade factors as covariates was therefore done for each of the eleven syntactic subtests.[3] Table 7 presents the F-ratios for the adjusted cell means and equality of slopes[4] of the eleven syntactic subtest scores for each Piagetian task.

When Table 7 is compared to Table 4 it is evident that operational level is still highly significant for many of the syntactic subtests, even when the effects of curriculum and grade are statistically removed. This is especially true for numeration, conservation of mass, and conservation of weight. Seriation and conservation of volume, however, produced relatively few significant F's when compared to the other three tasks. As pointed out previously, these two tasks did not discriminate the subject sample very well (see Table 3).

In summary, children classified as operational on the numeration, conservation of mass, and conservation of weight tasks performed significantly better than non-operational children on most syntactic comprehension tests when the effects of grade and curriculum were statistically removed. For the above three Piagetian tasks, twenty-four out of thirty-three independent analyses of covariance confirmed this prediction. If the number of significant F's is taken as an indication of how closely related operational reasoning is to performance on syntactic comprehension tests, it seems that the numeration task is most closely related to syntactic comprehension in both languages.

The curriculum factor. Because operational level was significant for several analyses of covariance of the English subtest scores, and because children in the immersion curriculum were classified as operational more often than 75-minute children, it was possible that the significant main effect of curriculum for English inflectional categories and English syntactic structures was due to the confounding of the curriculum and operational factors. That is, it was possible that increased exposure to French as defined by the intensity factor (curriculum) did not actually facilitate comprehension of English, but that the apparent facilitative effect was due to 'smarter' children being selected for the immersion program.

In order to isolate the effect of the curriculum factor on the comprehension of English syntax, a one-way analysis of covariance using the curriculum factor as the independent variable and the grade and operational factors as covariates was done. Table 8 presents the F-ratios for the adjusted cell means and equality of slopes of the three English subtest scores for the curriculum factor. When the effects of operational level and grade were controlled, the immersion group was significantly better than the 75-minute group only on the English syntactic structures subtest. The significant differences found for English

TABLE 7. Analysis of covariance F-ratios for equality of adjusted group means and equality of slopes of eleven syntactic subtest scores for the operational factor on five Piagetian tasks (covariates: curriculum and grade)

Subtest	Seriation F		Numeration F		Mass F		Weight F		Volume F	
	adj M	slope	adj M	slope	adj M	slope	adj M	slope	adj M	slope
1. EI	3.27	1.04	1.10	3.31*	4.74	4.71*	1.07	1.70	1.51	.20
2. ESS	1.41	1.39	9.38**	.55	17.93**	.62	6.67*	.95	3.25	.77
3. ESY	9.30**	.81	4.95*	2.77	6.83*	.57	.38	.94	.41	.65
4. FI	5.60*	.05	31.08**	.85	7.36**	.92	5.00	4.93*	6.67*	1.12
5. FSS	9.38**	1.36	7.40**	2.59	5.40*	2.69	5.26*	.77	4.55*	1.09
6. FSY	1.26	1.62	7.09*	3.03	1.24	1.58	2.80	4.85*	2.19	1.76
7. A-S	.77	.71	9.32**	1.66	4.84*	.57	6.24*	.91	2.17	1.83
8. A-V	.26	1.58	4.22*	2.78	1.03	1.29	4.34*	1.60	1.66	1.07
9. CE	5.50*	.89	9.47**	1.11	19.71**	1.39	4.67*	1.35	3.05	1.96
10. CF	9.10**	.63	20.93**	.19	7.49**	.49	7.19**	1.76	7.17**	1.78
11. CA	.01	.45	8.41**	1.44	3.05	1.01	7.03*	1.70	2.52	1.83

df (equality of adjusted group means) = 1/56
df (equality of slopes) = 2/54
*p < .05
**p < .01

TABLE 8. Analysis of covariance F-ratios for equality of adjusted group means and equality of slopes of three English subtest scores for the curriculum factor (covariates: grade and operational level on five Piagetian tasks)

English subtest	Seriation F		Numeration F		Mass F		Weight F		Volume F	
	adj M	slope	adj M	slope	adj M	slope	adj M	slope	adj M	slope
1. EI	2.54	1.33	3.48	2.74	3.88	3.29*	3.87	2.53	3.98	1.41
2. ESS	6.44*	.38	4.95*	.27	7.11**	.38	6.19*	.61	8.97**	.50
3. ESY	.24	2.07	.74	.19	1.29	.05	1.59	1.07	2.05	.74

df (equality of adjusted means) = 1/56
df (equality of slopes) = 2/54
*p < .05
**p < .01

inflectional categories in the previous analysis disappeared in the analysis of covariance.

The grade factor. Although the grade factor was found to be highly significant for each of the three English subtests, it was possible that this factor was confounded with the operational factor. In order to isolate the effect of the grade factor, a one-way analysis of covariance using grade as the independent variable and the operational and curriculum factors as covariates was done.

Table 9 presents the F-ratios for the adjusted cell means and equality of slopes of the three English subtest scores for the grade factor. Grade was still significant in every case except for English inflectional categories when curriculum and operational level on the conservation of mass task were controlled.

Post hoc Scheffé contrasts were calculated between the means of each two grades for the analyses which produced a significant F. Table 10 presents the significance levels for contrasts of the adjusted group means from the analyses of covariance for the grade factor. Fewer contrasts between the adjusted group means were significant than between the unadjusted group means. The pattern of significant contrasts for English syntactic structures, however, remained the same.

TABLE 9. Analysis of covariance F-ratios for equality of adjusted group means and equality of slopes of three English subtest scores for the grade factor (covariates: curriculum and operational level on five Piagetian tasks)

English subtest	Piagetian task									
	Seriation		Numeration		Mass		Weight		Volume	
	F		F		F		F		F	
	adj M	slope	adj M	slope	adj M	slope	adj M	slope	adj M	slope
1. EI	6.47**	.74	4.37*	.92	3.07	1.15	7.78**	.79	7.33**	#
2. ESS	32.69**	1.36	17.32**	1.01	18.56**	1.10	33.69**	.66	32.13**	#
3. ESY	30.30**	1.13	21.90**	.29	18.67**	.21	36.04**	.76	35.40**	#

df (equality of adjusted means) = 2/55
df (equality of slopes) = 4/51
*p < .05
**p < .01
#F-ratio not computed because the variance-covariance matrix for Grade One was singular (i.e. all Grade One subjects were non-operational on the volume task).

TABLE 10. Significance levels for contrasts between adjusted group means from the analyses of covariance of three English subtest scores for the grade factor (covariates: curriculum and operational level on five Piagetian tasks)

Contrast between grades	Piagetian task														
	Seriation			Numberation			Mass			Weight			Volume		
	1,3	2,3	1,2	1,3	2,3	1,2	1,3	2,3	1,2	1,3	2,3	1,2	1,3	2,3	1,2
English subtest															
1. EI	*	ns	ns	*	ns	*				**	ns	ns	**	ns	ns
2. ESS	**	**	**	**	**	**	**	**	*	**	**	**	**	**	**
3. ESY	**	ns	**	**	ns	**	**	ns	**	**	ns	**	**	ns	**

*p < .05
**p < .01

Factor analysis

The data were analyzed by submitting the intercorrelation matrix of twenty-two variables (excluding the three cumulative scores--see Table 2) to a principal components/principal axis factor analysis with varimax rotation. [5] The results of the factor analysis are presented in Table 11. Factor loadings of .40 and above were considered significant in interpreting the factors.

Factor I was identified as a maturation or time factor. Twelve variables loaded .40 or higher on this factor, with grade (.90) and chronological age (.89) having the highest loadings. The other ten significant variables were numeration and conservation of mass for both scoring methods, and six of the eight syntactic comprehension subtests. The significant loadings from the majority of the syntactic subtests and operational thought for two of the Piagetian tasks, as well as the time indices, logically suggested that Factor I represented abilities which unfold in time, or abilities which have been described as due to maturation. The fact that syntactic comprehension and operational thought both loaded on this factor suggested that the abilities necessary for the comprehension of syntax were the same abilities required for demonstration of operational thinking, at least for numeration and conservation of mass.

TABLE 11. Varimax rotation of factor pattern for twenty-two variables

Variable	Factors					
	I	II	III	IV	V	VI
Sex	-.01	.02	-.10	-.05	.04	.94
Grade	.90	.14	-.01	.08	.20	-.05
Curriculum	-.16	.82	.03	.24	-.11	-.03
Ser. Level	.17	.16	.17	.91	.05	-.06
Num. Level	.56	.36	.38	.19	.11	.24
Mass Level	.62	.09	.62	.18	-.02	-.02
Weight Level	.07	.22	.78	.08	.35	-.19
Volume Level	.17	.05	.14	.03	.92	.07
Chron. Age	.89	.07	.02	.04	.17	.04
EI	.52	.15	.19	.37	.08	.02
ESS	.73	.35	.28	.09	.15	-.02
ESY	.73	.26	.11	.35	.11	-.03
FI	.41	.75	.21	.29	.17	.02
FSS	.52	.57	.19	.35	.15	-.05
FSY	.39	.67	.10	.18	.17	.08
A-S	.24	.75	.34	-.10	.05	.08
A-V	.50	.70	.12	.09	.17	-.07
Ser. Score	.19	.17	.15	.92	.04	-.04
Num. Score	.48	.35	.41	.36	.07	.20
Mass Score	.47	.12	.66	.37	-.05	.06
Weight Score	-.02	.23	.82	.20	.30	-.05
Volume Score	.27	.13	.25	.07	.86	.01
% variance accounted for	29.03	21.06	16.40	15.95	11.53	6.02

Factor II was identified as a French curriculum factor, with significant loadings from six variables, the highest being curriculum (.82) and the other five being all subtests requiring comprehension of French. Factors I and II accounted for most of the variability of the linguistic measures, which did not load significantly on any of the remaining factors. Factor II suggested, perhaps obviously, that the amount of exposure to French as defined by the intensity factor (curriculum) had an effect on the comprehension of French. This effect evidently was unrelated to the time factor of the amount of exposure to French, as defined by grade.

It is interesting to note that French syntactic structures loaded almost as heavily on Factor I as on Factor II, suggesting that performance on this subtest was closely related to both maturation and exposure to French.

Factor III was clearly an operational thought factor, with significant loadings from five Piagetian measures. At first glance, it may be surprising to find that neither of the two time indices loaded significantly on Factor III, since it has often been stressed that operational thought is mainly determined by 'maturation'. Nonetheless, a review of the loadings on Factor III indicates that operational thought may represent abilities which are to some degree independent of the passage of time in childhood. This interpretation is supported by numerous studies which have shown that the age of attaining concrete operational thought on a particular task can vary between children by as much as three or four years, which was the age range of this subject sample.

Factors IV, V, and VI were defined by significant loadings from seriation, conservation of volume, and sex variables, respectively. Interpretation of these factors was similar. Previous analyses showed that the variability in performance on seriation and conservation of volume was very small, and the sex factor was not significant for any of the syntactic measures. Therefore, it was not surprising that Factors IV, V, and VI, identified as the seriation, conservation of volume, and sex factors respectively, accounted for little but their own variance. That is, no variables loaded .40 or above on Factor IV except measures of seriation, on Factor V except measures of volume conservation, and on Factor VI except sex differences.

Analyses of the pattern of errors

Performance of balanced bilinguals. The major purpose of this analysis was to replicate with English-French bilingual children Kessler's findings with Italian-English bilingual children. Only the performance of a subset of the total sample of this study was applicable, that is, children in the first two grades with a mean age of about seven years, standard deviation about .75, whose cumulative scores for the two languages were highly correlated (i.e. cumulative French and cumulative English scores).

As the criterion for 'balanced bilingualism', subjects in Grades One and Two, immersion, and 75-minute classes, whose cumulative French and cumulative English scores differed by no more than four points were selected. There were sixteen such subjects. Table 12 presents the number of subjects within each sex, grade, and curriculum which were considered balanced bilinguals according to the above criterion. The mean age for this group was 7.37 years, standard deviation .52. Therefore, the subjects of this sub-sample were in general older by a few months than the subjects of Kessler's sample.

TABLE 12. Number of balanced bilinguals by sex, grade, and curriculum

	Grade One		Grade Two	
	male	female	male	female
75-minute curriculum	1	1	1	0
Immersion curriculum	3	2	4	4
Total	4	3	5	4

The total number of errors made by the balanced bilinguals was tabulated for each linguistic structure within each subtest. These results, as well as Kessler's results for her twelve subjects, are presented for inflectional categories (Table 13), and syntactic structures (Table 14). Kessler's results were compared to the results of this study for the sequenced order of difficulty of these structures, not for the absolute number of errors.

Table 13 shows that the balanced bilinguals of this sample found comprehension of English inflectional categories much easier than the subjects of Kessler's sample. Only verb tense was not fully understood. Therefore the relative difficulty of the other five categories, where almost no errors were made, could not meaningfully be compared to Kessler's findings. In the French test for inflectional categories, however, it was surprising to find that pronoun gender and possessive adjective number were poorly differentiated.

TABLE 13. Number of errors per inflectional category for balanced bilinguals on English and French, and on English from Kessler's study

	English	French	Kessler's English
No. of items per structure	64	74	72
Verb tense	13*	8*	34
Pronoun obj. (gen.)	1	19	10
Poss. adj. (no.)	1	11	12
Verb person	0	8	16
Noun gender	0	0	2
Noun number	0	0	1

*Verb tense was tested by means of six, not four, items. These error scores are adjusted for comparison with other categories by multiplying by 2/3.

TABLE 14. Number of errors per syntactic structure for balanced bilinguals on English and French, and on English from Kessler's study

	English	French	Kessler's English
No. of items per structure	64	64	72
1. For-to	46	48	54
Obj. inversion (English-spec.)	--	--	48
2. Dir./Ind. obj.	29	21	12*
3. Reflex/recipr.	24	25	29
4. Passive	17	19	29
5. Rel. clause	6	4	24
6. Poss. X of Y	4	2	24
7. Comparative adj.	1	4	19
8. From-to	2	2	16
9. Noun/adjective	0	0	16
Dir./Ind. obj. (verb 'bring' only)	0**	0**	--
10. Subj./Ind. obj.	0	0	11
11. Active	0	0	22*

*Structures out of sequence according to the results of the present study.
**These results were included in the list in order to show that structure 2 (Dir./Ind. obj.) errors were due entirely to items with the verb 'show'.

Of major interest to the study was the sequenced order of difficulty of the syntactic structures of French and English. The pattern of errors made by the balanced bilingual subjects showed a remarkable consistency between French and English. The only noticeable deviation was the direct/indirect object structure, where it appeared to be slightly more difficult in English. Except for two structures (direct/indirect object and the active), the order of difficulty closely approximated Kessler's findings.

The balanced bilinguals of this sample performed better on the English syntactic structures and English inflectional categories subtests than did Kessler's subjects. The structures labelled 7 to 11 in Table 14 were almost perfectly understood.

Performance of the balanced bilinguals on the auditory subtests are presented in Table 15 for synonymous sentences within languages and Table 16 for the across-languages test. These results were not directly compared to Kessler's for several reasons. First, the subtests were greatly shortened, with only two items per structure, so that only the total score of each subtest was

TABLE 15. Number of errors per syntactic variant for balanced bilinguals on the English and French subtests of synonymous sentences within languages

	English	French
No. of items per structure	32	32
Syntactic variant		
active/passive	10	11
passive/active	6	7
rel. cl./adjective	6	2 —
np/obj. pronoun	2	6 —
poss. np/np	2	3
Total	26	29

TABLE 16. Number of errors per structure for balanced bilinguals on the across-languages test

	Similar structures		Syntactic variants	
No. of items per structure	32		32	
	subj. pro.	7	pass./act.	10
	rel. cl.	4	act./pass.	6
	act./pass.	4	np/subj. pro.	5
	obj. pro.	3	np/obj. pro.	5
			rel. cl./adj.	4
			poss. np/np	3
	Total	18	Total	33

felt to be interpretable. Second, the method of presenting these tests differed radically from Kessler's method. Finally, the structures tested did not differ much in difficulty so that there were no good grounds for attempting to sequence them. One striking difference between the results of this study and Kessler's results for the auditory tests was that the subjects of this sample found the tests much easier. For example, on the synonymous sentences within languages tests, Kessler's sample performed at about 50 percent accuracy, whereas the subjects of this sample performed at about 80 percent accuracy.

Similarly, the subjects of this sample were about 85 percent accurate on the across languages, similar structures, test (Kessler's--75 percent), and 83 percent accurate on the syntactic variants across languages (Kessler's--70 percent). Nonetheless, these percentages must be interpreted with caution because of the small number of subjects.

Performance by grade and curriculum. In this section, the number of errors per structure for the total sample is analyzed by grade and curriculum. The major purpose of this analysis was to replicate Kessler's analyses for a larger number of subjects from a wider age range and to investigate the possibility that, when French is the weaker language, the sequencing of structures by difficulty would approximate the pattern found for balanced bilinguals.

Figure 1 shows the number of errors made by the total sample on inflectional categories in English and French. Except for verb tense, English inflections were almost perfectly differentiated, as was found for the balanced bilinguals. Comprehension of French inflections, on the other hand, was very poor by comparison. Figure 2, showing the number of errors in French inflectional categories by grade and curriculum, suggested that the poor comprehension of French inflectional categories in Figure 1 was due to the performance of subjects who had little exposure to French (e. g. the Grade One, immersion subjects and the subjects in the 75-minute curriculum).

FIGURE 1. Number of errors in English and French inflectional categories for the total sample

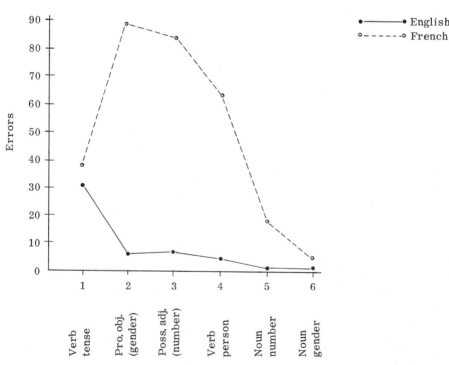

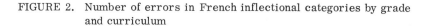

FIGURE 2. Number of errors in French inflectional categories by grade and curriculum

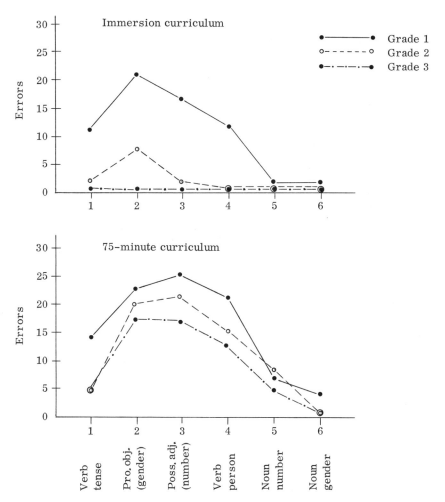

Figure 3 shows the errors in English and French syntactic structures for the total sample. The sequencing of English syntactic structures by difficulty for the total sample was identical to the results for the balanced bilinguals. The relative difficulty of the eleven English syntactic structures was therefore confirmed for a wider age range. As noted for balanced bilinguals, the results for the total sample also place the direct/indirect object structure and the active structure out of sequence when compared with Kessler's results. When performance on English syntactic structures was broken down by grade and curriculum (Figure 4), the sequences were approximately the same, except perhaps for the passive which was more difficult for the Grade One immersion subjects.

When errors made by the total sample for syntactic structures were compared between French and English (Figure 3), the sequence of structures for

FIGURE 3. Number of errors in English and French syntactic structures for
the total sample

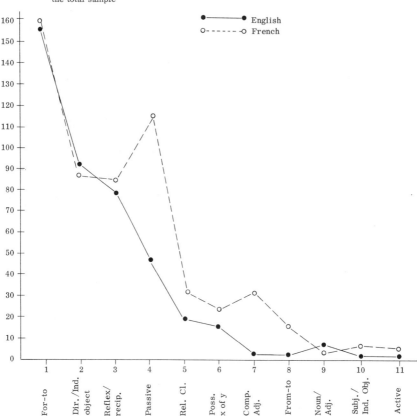

both languages was approximately the same, except for the passive and comparative adjective. The greater difficulty of these two structures in French required
clarification. Figure 5 shows the number of errors in French syntactic structures broken down by grade and curriculum.

It is evident from Figure 5 that the 75-minute group and the Grade One
immersion group made the errors which accounted for the large differences
between the English and French sequences observed in Figure 3. Figure 5
also revealed that Grade Two immersion subjects made several more errors
than any other group on the reflexive/reciprocal structure.

For the reasons stated above regarding the balanced bilingual group, no
attempt was made to sequence by difficulty the structures tested in the auditory
subtests for the total sample. Only the total number of errors on each subtest
was felt to be interpretable, and these are presented by grade and curriculum
for synonymous sentences in both languages (Figure 6) and for the across-
languages subtests (Figure 7).

Figure 6 shows that performance of the two curricula groups was very
much the same for English synonymous sentences, a finding which was confirmed by the statistical analyses reported above (Tables 5 and 8).

FIGURE 4. Number of errors in English syntactic structures by grade and curriculum

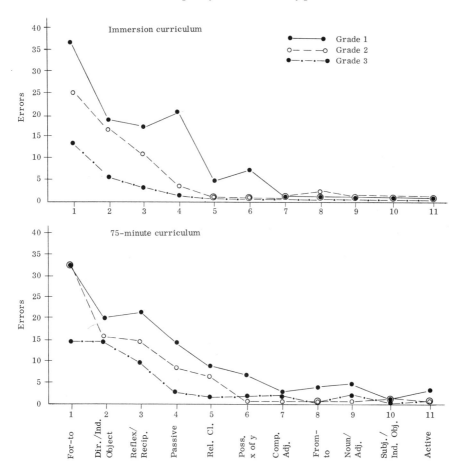

Performance on French synonymous sentences, on the other hand, was better by the immersion group, especially in Grades Two and Three. Figure 7 shows the same trend even more strongly. Performance on similar structures across languages improved hardly at all over the grades in the 75-minute group when compared to the immersion group. Similarly, performance on syntactic variants across languages improved much faster over the grades in the immersion group.

Performance by operational level. The statistical analyses for the operational factor dealt with the total scores for the subtests only. In this section, the pattern of errors is contrasted between operational and non-operational children for those subtests which allowed sequencing of structures by difficulty, that is, English and French syntactic structures and French inflectional categories. Operational level on the numeration, conservation of mass, and conservation of weight tasks only were contrasted, since these three tasks were significant most often for the syntactic measures.

FIGURE 5. Number of errors in French syntactic structures by grade and curriculum

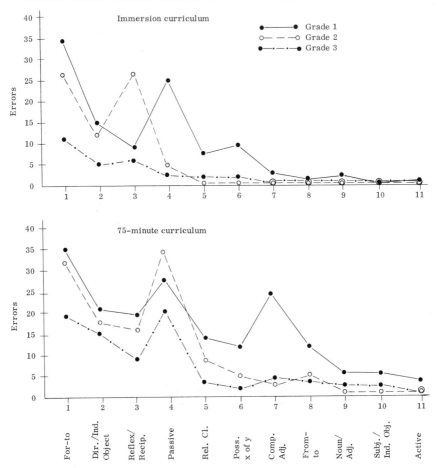

Performance on the English inflectional categories subtest was not contrasted between operational and non-operational children because the structures of this subtest were almost perfectly differentiated except for verb
tense, and therefore did not allow a meaningful sequencing by difficulty.
Similarly, performance on the auditory subtests was not contrasted between
operational and non-operational children because the structures tested could
not meaningfully be sequenced. In any case, information on the relationship
of operational level and total scores on the auditory subtests can be obtained
from Table 7.

Figures 8, 9, and 10 show the mean number of errors in English and
French syntactic structures for operational and non-operational children on
the numeration, conservation of mass, and conservation of weight tasks,
respectively. The large number of errors on the passive and comparative
adjective structures in French which were found for the total sample

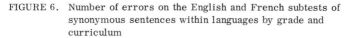

FIGURE 6. Number of errors on the English and French subtests of synonymous sentences within languages by grade and curriculum

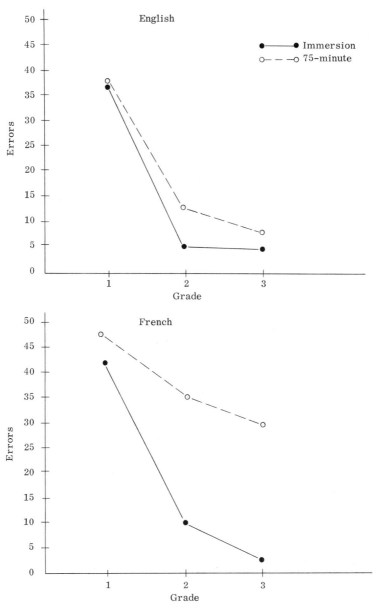

FIGURE 7. Number of errors on the across-languages subtests by grade
and curriculum

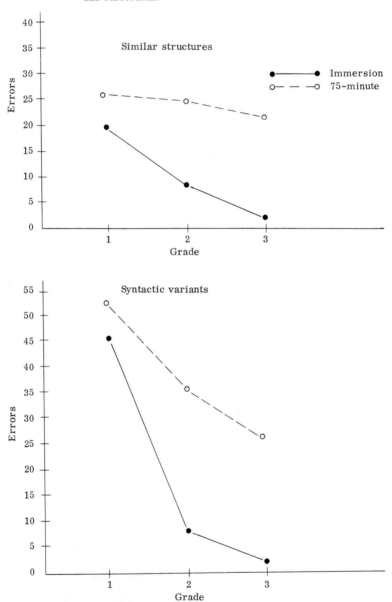

FIGURE 8. Mean number of errors in English and French syntactic structures for operational and non-operational children on the numeration task

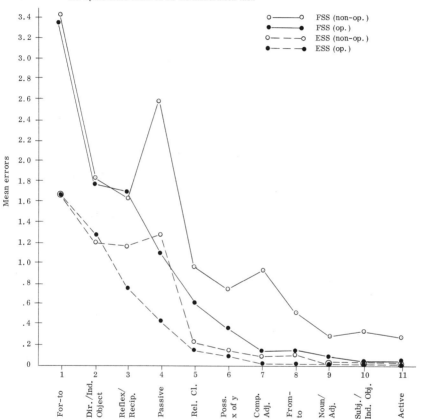

(Figure 3) is closely related to the performance of non-operational children, especially on the numeration task (Figure 8). Figure 9 reveals that non-operational children on the conservation of mass task generally made more errors in English than operational children made in French. A study of the three figures together shows that the conservation of mass and weight tasks were able to distinguish performance on the for-to structure by operational level, while the numeration task could not. That is, operational children on the mass and weight tasks tended to make much fewer errors on the for-to structure in both English and French.

Figure 11 shows the mean number of errors in French inflectional categories for operational and non-operational children on the numeration, conservation of mass, and conservation of weight tasks. When Figure 1 and Figure 11 are compared, it is clear that even the operational children

performed much worse on French inflectional categories than the total sample
did on English inflectional categories.

FIGURE 9. Mean number of errors in English and French syntactic structures for operational
and non-operational children on the conservation of mass task

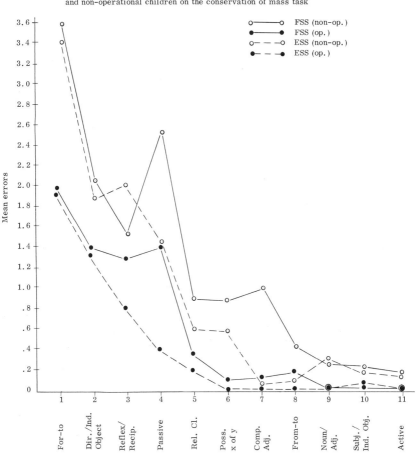

NOTES

1. The SOUPAC BALANOVA 5 computer program was used for these
analyses.

2. Hereafter, the eleven syntactic subtests will be abbreviated in the
tables as follows: English inflectional categories (EI); English syntactic
structures (ESS); English synonymous sentences (ESY); French inflectional
categories (FI); French syntactic structures (FSS); French synonymous sentences (FSY); across languages, similar structures (A-S); across languages,
syntactic variants (A-V); cumulative English (CE); cumulative French (CF);
and cumulative across languages (CA).

3. The BMD X 82 computer program was used for all analyses of covariance reported in this section.

FIGURE 10. Mean number of errors in English and French syntactic structures for operational and non-operational children on the conservation of weight task

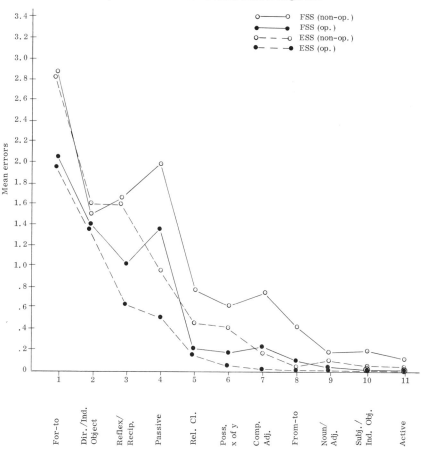

4. One assumption of the analysis of covariance is that the slope of the regression line is the same for all groups. When the F-ratio for slope is significant, therefore, the F-ratio for equality of means cannot be interpreted. This was the case for four analyses in Table 7--English inflectional categories for Numeration and Mass, French inflectional categories and French synonymous sentences for Weight.

5. The SOUPAC computer program was used for this analysis.

FIGURE 11. Mean number of errors in French inflectional categories for operational and non-operational children on the numeration, conservation of mass, and conservation of weight tasks.

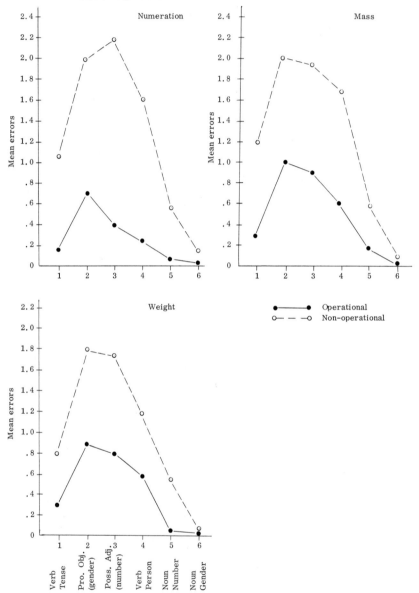

CHAPTER FOUR

SYNTAX-'LEARNING' REINTERPRETED

Syntax as one instance of operational intelligence. Before the results regarding the major hypotheses of the study are discussed, some clarification
is needed about the limitations of the research design used and, especially,
about the implications of Piagetian tests as measures of intelligence.

Circumstances were such that the data were gathered in a way which did
not strictly conform to an ideal experimental model. That is, no experimental
'treatments' were imposed on the subjects, such as, for example, applying
more than two levels of exposure to French (intensity), ranging from zero to
some strictly controlled intermediate level to total immersion. Ideally, the
subjects would be randomly assigned to each of the three treatment groups at
the beginning of the year in Grade One, and would be tested at the end of the
school year until Grade Three. Such a design was not possible within the
Ottawa Roman Catholic Separate School Board at the time the study was conducted, but perhaps it would be possible in other contexts. Similarly, it was
not possible to select an adequate number of operational and non-operational
children on each Piagetian task to satisfy the requirements of parametric
statistics, so that simultaneous analyses of variance could not be done for
all the independent variables with which this study was concerned. Nonetheless, it should be pointed out that the two major hypotheses for which statistical analyses were appropriate (see the section 'Design and hypotheses')
were exploratory in that, as far as can be seen from the literature, no previous studies have tested them using linguistic measures based on case grammar. In view of the novelty of the study, statistically significant findings can
be interpreted as at least suggestive that the predictions have been confirmed
even when the design limitations mentioned above are taken into account.

In a sense, then, this study was correlational in that causal effects could
not be strictly inferred for the curriculum factor. As will be seen, however,
it would not have made sense to postulate causal relationships for most of the
problems investigated.

The focus of the study was the investigation of cognitive abilities which
have been called maturational. Both syntax and Piagetian intelligence fit
under this rubric. It was postulated that competence in both these realms
springs from the same abilities and therefore it was hypothesized that dramatic improvement in one realm would be accompanied by a similar improvement in the other. Since the evidence to date suggests that certain aspects

of the syntax of two languages are not encoded separately, it seemed reasonable to hypothesize that the syntax of both languages in the bilingual child would improve with operational intelligence.

The use of Piagetian tasks to measure intelligence affords many advantages over standardized tests of intelligence such as I. Q. indices because of the way operational thought develops. I. Q. is based on the concept of mental age (MA) which increases as a linear function of age until about age eighteen. In fact, the items used to measure MA were selected so that they would discriminate children at one-year intervals. In other words, originally these items were chosen on an 'intuitive' basis of what constitutes intelligence, that is, by common sense notions. At the same time, items which did not discriminate children at one-year intervals were dropped. If cognitive development is conceived in terms of MA, maturation is seen as gradual improvement in performance until about the age of eighteen. If an MA index had been used as a measure of cognitive development to be related to syntax, no conclusions could have been reached regarding maturational processes. Naturally, MA would improve with age and so would syntactic performance, and significant differences between any two selected 'levels' would be completely unrevealing in a study such as the present one in which the intention was to investigate those processes which underlie maturational abilities.

Operational intelligence, on the other hand, does not improve as a linear function of age. A plateau period where performance on Piagetian tasks does not change is followed by sudden and rapid improvement at about age seven, after which little improvement is evident until about age thirteen, when again dramatic improvement occurs.

The difference in intelligence between operational and non-operational children, therefore, is not a minor difference. It represents a major change in the way the child understands, interprets, and perceives (Piaget and Inhelder 1971) his experience. The subjects of this study were selected so that their age range would straddle the well-documented average age of the onset of concrete operations. A significant difference in syntactic performance between children at these two levels of cognitive development is therefore much more revealing for a theory of maturational abilities than a difference between two MA levels. For example, such a difference would imply that the rules and learning processes descriptive of concrete operational thought may also be descriptive of the syntax of operational children. At the present time, developmental psycholinguists need more information about the nature of syntax and how it is learned. A demonstration that various aspects of operational thought and syntax are closely related would be revealing for a theory of how syntax is learned. It should be noted that, while syntactic development is poorly understood, a detailed, integrated theory with supporting research exists about the development of operational intelligence. In this study, it was hoped that this wealth of theoretical and experimental knowledge could help illuminate the problem of language acquisition.

The results strongly suggested that when children learning a second language reach the stage of concrete operations, comprehension of the syntax of both their native and their second language improves greatly. In sixty-two out of sixty-five independent analyses of variance for the operational factor, it was found that children classified as operational performed significantly better in both languages than children classified as non-operational.

When the effects of grade and curriculum were controlled, the operational factor was still highly significant in most instances, although the number of significant analyses for operational level on seriation and conservation of volume was reduced. As noted previously, the number of non-operational subjects on the seriation task was very small by comparison with other tasks, and the number of operational subjects on the volume task was also very small by comparison. These two tasks, therefore, were either too hard or too easy for the age group chosen, unlike numeration, conservation of mass, and conservation of weight which allowed classification of approximately equal numbers of subjects into the two categories.

For the age range of the subject sample, it seems that the seriation and volume tasks do not discriminate performance on syntactic comprehension as well as the other three tasks, as the analyses of covariance and the factor analysis suggested. Nonetheless, further research is needed using younger subjects for the seriation task and older subjects for the volume task in order to decide whether these two tasks are in fact less strongly related to syntactic comprehension than numeration, conservation of mass and weight.

The factor analysis results suggest that abilities needed to solve the problems posed by the numeration, mass, and weight tasks are the same abilities needed for the comprehension of syntax, and that these abilities are maturational, or are closely related to chronological age and grade. Nonetheless, factor analysis also suggested that operational intelligence may be somewhat independent of linguistic abilities in that they are not as closely related to time indices. Factor 3 and the intercorrelation matrix suggested such an interpretation.

One interesting finding of the study was that the numeration task seemed to be more strongly related to syntactic comprehension in both languages than any other task used. Even when the effects of grade and curriculum were statistically removed, operational children on the numeration task were significantly better than non-operational children on ten of the eleven syntactic measures. In the factor analysis, measures of this task together with most of the syntactic variables loaded more heavily on the maturation factor than on any other factor. This close association of syntactic comprehension and numeration abilities seems surprising at first glance, but not when one considers the nature of the numeration task. The child was required to reason about a seriated set of objects, and at the same time impose a hierarchy on the series. The analytic properties of syntax for the comprehension of the speech stream are very similar. That is, to understand what is said, the listener must impose a hierarchical structure (syntax) on a series of meaningful units which unfold in time.

In order to test Lambert and Tucker's (1972) suggestion that children with more exposure to French would be better at English, the performance of children with different degrees of exposure to French was compared on the English syntactic subtests. In general, children in higher grades performed better than children in lower grades as would be expected, especially on the English syntactic structures subtest. The interesting finding was that children in the immersion curriculum were significantly better on the English syntactic structures subtest only, after the effects of grade and operational level were statistically controlled. It seems, therefore, that intensive exposure to French improves the comprehension of English syntax when it is defined in terms of case grammar.

Although grade level was treated as a French exposure factor, its significant effect on English syntax did not interact with the curriculum factor. This suggests that abilities which unfold in time, as indicated by grade level, are independent of the effects of intensive exposure to a second language on the syntactic comprehension of the native language. The factor analysis, which included the French subtests as well, also suggested that abilities which unfold in time are to some extent independent of intensity factors.

A superficial consideration of these results may suggest that the maturational factor, represented by grade and operational level, can be contrasted with the intensity factor which in turn could be called 'environmental or training effects'. In other words, the age-old distinction between maturational and environmental influences on cognitive abilities would be confirmed. Further, it could be argued along these lines that, because both grade level and operational level were highly correlated with chronological age, the significant effects of these two factors were simply due to maturation as defined by chronological age.

The term 'maturation' has often been applied to the passage of time in childhood, yet the passage of time in itself cannot be an explanatory principle, although it can be a predictive tool when rendered in terms of age. But to say that changes observed during childhood were due to maturation is meaningless if maturation is defined solely in terms of age or grade level. As pointed out above regarding MA, the major interest of the study was the investigation of maturational processes, not the prediction of changes from indices of maturation, such as time indices. In other words, this study sought to describe those abilities which unfold in time in terms which are more revealing than chronological age.

Within this framework, it is a highly significant finding that the comprehension of English syntactic structures was facilitated by intensive exposure to French because English syntactic structures had a loading of .73 on the maturational factor, and did not load significantly on any other factor including the French intensity factor. This suggests that syntax, seen within the context of case grammar, is a maturational ability which can be influenced by 'training'. [For a fuller discussion of case grammar, see sections 1.0-2.3 of Appendix A.] This interpretation is further supported by the fact that French syntactic structures loaded significantly and almost equally on the maturational and French intensity factors (.52 and .57 respectively).

The significant effect of intensive training in French on the comprehension of English syntax may have been due to the age range of the subjects tested. In Piagetian research the attainment of concrete operations can be accelerated by training only when children are about to discover these concepts themselves, that is, around the age of six to eight. Further research is needed to test the possibility that intensive exposure to French would not facilitate comprehension of English syntax in children both younger and older than the subjects tested in this study.

These results suggest that the facilitative effect on English syntax by exposure to French was only possible because the syntax of these two languages have underlying similarities or, in linguistic terminology, share universal deep structure, and therefore intensive exposure to one language could affect comprehension of the other language. Further, the factor analysis results suggest that this universal deep structure shared by the two languages may be considered the same ability as some aspects of operational intelligence.

It is possible, therefore, that the maturation of these two characteristically human abilities can be described in the same terms. Operational intelligence appears to be invulnerable to training except at certain crucial ages. Further research is needed to investigate this possibility with syntactic development, although the study was able to show that in the age range when operational thought is trainable, syntactic comprehension was also. Another interesting problem which this study was not able to investigate was the possibility that the operational level was affected by intensive exposure to French. If operational thought and syntax stem from the same abilities, and if English syntax can be facilitated by intensive exposure to French, then of course it is possible that concrete operations would be accelerated by intensive exposure of English-speaking children to French.

Although the rationale for relating operational intelligence to the comprehension of syntax was originally based on the observation that equilibration in Piagetian theory and 'rule stabilization' in psycholinguistics are very similar concepts, it would be going far beyond the data gathered in this study to state that the acquisition of syntax is governed by a learning principle such as equilibration. Nonetheless, the results discussed above do suggest such a possibility. Experimental work now needs to be done to explain the demonstrated close relationship of syntax and operational thought in development. Perhaps research on equilibration as a learning principle in syntactic development, using a design similar to the one used by Silverman and Geiringer (1973) for operational thought, would shed light on this problem.

It seems that research in the area of maturational abilities will have to be guided by new theories of what constitutes learning. As suggested above. changes in human cognitive abilities such as syntactic comprehension and operational intelligence during childhood may be governed by 'learning' principles which are yet to be formulated, but which may resemble equilibration. If learning is defined in terms of change in the organization of mental structures[1] and not in terms of environmental effects, if in fact environmental effects could be defined independently of the characteristics of the organism which is affected, then no paradox is encountered by the term 'maturational learning'. 'Process' theory in psycholinguistics would have some basis upon which to build a theory of language learning.

Error patterns in syntactic comprehension during development

Kessler's study demonstrated that the development of syntax in a small sample of balanced English-Italian bilingual children followed the same pattern in both languages. That is, the order and rate of acquiring syntactic structures shared by the two languages was approximately the same. In the present study, the performance of a selected subsample of 'balanced' English-French bilingual children as well as children whose French was weaker than English generally confirmed Kessler's findings.

When English syntactic structures were sequenced by difficulty, the sequences were identical for the balanced bilingual group and the total sample which included children whose French was the weaker language. It seems, therefore, that increased competence in a second language does not affect the relative difficulty of syntactic structures in the native language. This particular sequence was approximately the same as the one found by Kessler, although not identical. When the relative difficulty of these structures was compared between English and French, once again the sequences showed remarkable consistency for the balanced bilingual group. Children consistently made more errors in comprehending structures which involved rank shift in the hierarchy of cases, complex embedding, and co-referentiality contrasts than they did in comprehending structures which involved simple case relations. [Case hierarchy, complex embedding, and co-referentiality are discussed in more detail in Appendix A.] These findings definitely suggest that case grammar is a felicitous tool for describing the broad outlines of syntactic development. Nonetheless it is a tool which needs refining. In Kessler's study and in the present one, case grammar theory was used for selecting and describing the syntactic structures tested, although it is not possible from the present state of the theory to predict which of any two relatively complex structures would be more difficult for children to comprehend. For example, it was not possible to predict that the for-to contrast would be more difficult than the relative clause contrast, although it was possible to predict that the passive would be more difficult than the active. Developmental studies such as the present one can provide data for revising or supplementing a theory while at the same time taking their rationale and justification from the theory itself.

The two syntactic structures which were consistently out of sequence when compared with Kessler's results (the active and the direct/indirect object structures) can be considered in the light of theory supplementation. One could infer from case grammar theory, although not for any overwhelming reasons, that, from the set of syntactic structures tested, children between the ages of six and ten would find the active structure the easiest to comprehend. Such an inference was confirmed in the present study.

The results for the direct/indirect object structure, however, are more difficult to explain in terms of the theory. The surprising difficulty of this structure was noted during testing. Almost without exception, when errors were made on this structure, they were made to the contrast 'the girl shows the dog to the cow/the girl shows the cow to the dog'. When some of the children were questioned regarding their (incorrect) choice, they said, 'Well, the girl shows the dog the cow, doesn't she?', pointing to the wrong picture.

No errors at all were made in English with the same structure on the other two items ('the boy brings the mouse to the cat/the boy brings the cat to the mouse'), and only six errors were made in French for the total sample. It seemed clear that this structure was difficult because of some features related to the verb show. To test some hypotheses regarding these features, two additional items were inserted in the middle of the experiment, the English-specific direct/indirect object inversion tested by means of 'the boy shows the cat the bird/the boy shows the bird the cat'. Those children who made errors on the direct/indirect object structure almost without exception were correct on the object inversion items.

The explanation offered for this phenomenon is as follows, although further research is necessary to test it. As Kessler formulated it, the direct/indirect object is inserted in the case frame V[___AOSG]/A=S and the object inversion requires a rank shift of the O and G cases in the selection hierarchy for the surface object, thus making the object inversion structure more difficult, as Kessler found. [See Appendix A, sections 2.2, 2.4, 2.5, and 2.6.] However, the verb show in French and English may have associated with it an obligatory rank shift, at least in the languages spoken in the Ottawa area. Therefore the normal order of cases would be 'abnormal' for the verb show, producing the effects described above.

The only noticeable deviation between the English and French sequences for balanced bilinguals was the direct/indirect object structure, where it appeared to be slightly more difficult in English. This structure may have been more difficult because English, unlike French, has a surface reali- zation of what may be a deep structure rank shift (see Appendix A, section 2.6) for the verb show, that is, the direct/indirect object inversion, which may have served to further confuse the children in understanding this com- plex structure in English.

The performance of the total sample on French syntactic structures differed from the performance of the balanced bilinguals in that the passive and comparative adjective structures were much more difficult in French than in English. This error pattern for the total sample must have been due to those children who were not balanced bilinguals, that is, children whose French was weaker than English. Figure 5 suggests that French was weaker than English in the 75-minute curriculum and in the Grade One immersion group in that most of the errors made in the French passive and comparative adjective structures were made by these groups. Intuitively speaking, the Grade One immersion group and the 75-minute curriculum groups in all three grades were similar in that the immersion group had little exposure to French in terms of the time factor, and the 75-minute group had little exposure to French in terms of the intensity factor. If the Grade One immer- sion and the three 75-minute groups can be equated in this fashion, then their similar performance on the French inflectional categories subtest can also be explained. That is, these groups made numerous errors on the French inflectional categories subtest and these errors accounted for most of the difference between performance on the English and French inflectional cate- gories subtests for the total sample.

To recapitulate, by comparing the performance of the balanced bilinguals to the total sample and by applying 'subtractive' reasoning, it is possible to isolate the passive and comparative adjective as two structures which were poorly differentiated by children whose French was the weaker language. These children evidently were the youngest of the sample (Grade One), or they were in the 75-minute curriculum, and both these groups could be described as children with relatively little exposure to French.

It is not surprising therefore that children classified as non-operational also performed much worse on the French passive and comparative adjec- tive structures as well as on the French inflectional categories subtest than did operational children (see Figures 8, 9, 10, and 11). If our interpreta- tion is correct, that syntax is comprehended by the same abilities Piaget describes as operational intelligence and that 'training' or exposure to French may influence operational intelligence, then of course one would expect that non-operational children and children with little exposure to French would make the same kinds of errors in French. Statistically speaking, we are suggesting here that the curriculum and operational factors interact, an analysis which was not possible in this study because of the small numbers of subjects in the smallest cell of the three-factor matrix.

How exactly syntax and operational intelligence can be considered as identical is a question for further research, although some suggestions can be found in the results of this study. For example, because the conservation of mass and weight tasks could distinguish performance on the for-to struc- ture by operational level, it could be that those abilities necessary for understanding conservation of mass and weight are crucial for understanding rank shift in the hierarchy of cases in such instances as the for-to construction. [See Appendix A, section 2.6.]

During testing, the surprising difficulty of this structure was noticed, and it was decided to insert an additional contrast in the French syntactic structures subtest to test the possibility that the case frame in itself determined the difficulty of the for-to construction (V[__AOSG(B)]/A=S), not the rank shift in hierarchy of cases. A to-for contrast was inserted ('la mère montre le livre à la fille pour le garçon/la mère montre le livre au garçon pour la fille') at the same time during testing when the English-specific direct/indirect object inversion contrast was inserted. The children who were tested on the to-for contrast did much better on it than the for-to contrast. The difficulty of the to-for contrast was about equivalent to the difficulty of the subject/indirect object contrast--in other words, it seemed to be one of the easiest structures tested. [See Appendix A, 2.2, 2.6.]

These results suggested that it was rank shift in itself, not the complexity of the case frame, which the children found so difficult. Those who could conserve mass and weight found this structure much easier to comprehend, and this may have been due to the fact that reversibility principles must be grasped before children can show conservation. Comprehension of structures manifesting rank shift may have been easier for operational children because reversibility allows considering structures as identical even when certain aspects are transformed.

One puzzling finding which deserves discussion was that the Grade Two immersion group performed worse on the French reflexive/reciprocal contrast than any other group, including the Grade One 75-minute group (see Figure 5). No good explanation for this finding can be offered, although the contrast was especially difficult to represent in a picture and may have presented ambiguities. That is, in the contrast 'the girls see each other/the girls see themselves', the picture representing the girls seeing themselves in the mirror could also have been taken to represent the girls seeing each other in the mirror. To get the item correct, the child had to pay close attention to the eyes of the people in the pictures. In every other structure where a verb was used, the two contrasts were tested by means of different verbs, whereas the reflexive/reciprocal was tested with the same verb in both contrasts and the same situation was represented (looking in a mirror).

A change in the method of presenting the auditory tests and the drastic shortening of these tests did not allow a direct comparison with Kessler's findings nor a sequencing of the structures tested, a definite limitation of the study. Nonetheless, the auditory tests as a whole seemed to be easier for the subjects of this study than for the subjects of Kessler's study, perhaps due to the difference in test presentation, or to the fact that the balanced bilinguals of this study were somewhat older.

More research is needed to untangle the effects of the many complex processes tapped by the auditory tests. Research has only begun on the mental operations necessary for adults to match a sentence in their native language with a picture (Glucksberg, Trabasso, and Wald 1973), whereas the processes necessary for children to match a spoken sentence in one language with a transformed spoken sentence in another must involve many more complex operations. The difference in comprehension of synonymity from language A to language B, as opposed to comprehension from B to A, also needs to be researched with subjects whose second language is weaker.

Implications for theories of child bilingualism

The results of this study can provide data for theories of child bilingualism only in those aspects which concern comprehension, not production. Even those children who were considered balanced bilinguals in this study were certainly not fluent in expressing themselves in French, as the French tester noted several times during conversation with the subjects. Although previous research has shown that comprehension always precedes production (Fraser, Bellugi, and Brown 1963), the subjects of this study were atypical among other children who become bilingual in that they did not seem to practice speaking French except in the classroom. From casual observation in the schoolyard, it was noticed that English was the preferred language, and since most of the children came from English-speaking homes, one would expect that they did not practice French at home.

For comprehension ability only therefore, this study supported the L2=L1 hypothesis that bilingual children below the age of puberty will make the same kind of errors in both languages. This hypothesis is based on the assumption that languages at the deep structure level are very similar, and it is within its framework that the findings partially confirming Lambert and Tucker's hypothesis were explained. It seems that exposure to French facilitates the comprehension of a certain class of English syntactic structures in children between the ages of six and ten.

Even though it was found that French exposure appears to facilitate English comprehension, some anecdotal support for the contrastive analysis theory that negative transfer can occur between the two languages is offered, although this negative transfer occurred in the opposite direction than that predicted by the theory. In the auditory item 'the boy sees the flower: the boy sees it, the boy sees her', one subject said, 'It's her because it's little and so are girls'. It seems that this child had discovered some incomplete basis for making gender distinction in French and fancifully applied it incorrectly to English.

The results of this study suggested that the acquisition of both the first and second language is characterized by two learning phases. First, children appear to learn the normal hierarchy of cases which specify verbs, such as assigning which noun phrase in an utterance to which case. Then children learn exceptions to the normal hierarchy, such as transformations for rank shift. This second phase might entail appreciating signs marking cases out of their normal order. For example, the to-for construction was relatively easy for this subject sample, while the for-to construction was the most difficult of the ones tested. To suggest such a two-phase learning model is not new in the literature. For example, Ervin noted that children first appear to search for regularity in certain syntactic structures because once a rule is discovered, it is generalized to inappropriate contexts (i.e. foot-footiz, as in glass-glasses) so that even 'highly practiced, familiar plurals may be temporarily changed in form by overgeneralization of new patterns' (1964: 177). In a second phase, this overgeneralization is unlearned, and the child learns the exceptions to the rule. The pattern of learning new syntactic structures, therefore, might be searching for regularity first, discovering a rule, overgeneralizing the rule, and then, with enough experience of 'being wrong', adjusting the rule for exceptions. The role of experience, or exposure to language, can be seen as crucial at certain phases of learning. Comprehension of the French passive and comparative adjective discussed above could be one example.

It should be noted that a whole set of syntactic structures was tested in this study, and it was found that operational children comprehended these structures as a whole significantly better. Even when individual syntactic structures were isolated, operational children tended to perform better than non-operational children. This suggests that reaching the stage of concrete operations constituted a dramatic leap forward for a wide range of syntactic structures to be learned, not just for certain isolated ones.

During the age range of this sample, the normal hierarchy of cases appeared to be already learned, and the children seemed to be in the process of learning exceptions to rules. Exposure factors, therefore, would be crucial for improvement in the comprehension of both languages. Since exceptions to rules were being learned and since operational children improved in their comprehension of certain complex exceptions such as rank shift (see Appendix A, section 2.6), the stage of concrete operations may influence syntactic development in that new abilities for reordering and reclassifying units become available. Through reversibility principles, operational thought allows considering structures as identical even when their parts are regrouped or serially rearranged.

The close relationship of operational intelligence to syntactic comprehension must have been influenced by the way syntax was defined in this study. The verb is primary in case grammar, and Piagetian theory is based on the idea that intelligence develops from internalized action.

> The operations, such as the union of two classes (fathers united with mothers constitute parents) or the addition of two numbers, are <u>actions</u> characterized by their very great generality since the acts of uniting, arranging in order, etc., enter into all coordinations of particular actions. (Piaget and Inhelder 1969:96)

NOTE

1. A most successful synthesis of behaviorist learning theory and what is known of the changes in mental organization during psychotherapy has recently been published by Bateson (1972). This new theory was possible only by redefining the premises of the concept 'learning' in terms of change in the organization of mental structures, which in turn was defined in terms of cybernetics and systems theory.

CHAPTER FIVE

SUMMARY AND CONCLUSIONS

The close association of Piagetian operational thinking to syntactic development has been noted often by researchers concerned with the psychology of language, but almost no studies have been done directly relating these two cognitive realms systematically and in detail. The main interest of this study has been to investigate the possibility that concrete operational thought and the comprehension of syntax in the bilingual child are based on the same abilities. If this were the case, Piaget's theory, and the great volume of research supporting it, could be used to illuminate the problems of language acquisition.

Five Piagetian tasks varying in difficulty and syntactic comprehension tests in French and English, based on Kessler's methodology, were administered to English-speaking children in Grades One, Two, and Three, enrolled in either a French immersion curriculum or a curriculum which included 75 minutes of instruction in French per day. The design of the study allowed an investigation of Lambert and Tucker's suggestion that increased exposure to a second language may facilitate competence in the native language, and a replication of Kessler's study of English-Italian bilingual children.

The results indicated that, when the stage of concrete operations is reached, the comprehension of both English and French improves greatly, even when the effects of grade and curriculum are controlled. Factor analytic results suggested further that syntactic comprehension and certain aspects of operational thought constitute the same abilities. These results were interpreted to mean that new abilities which define concrete operational intelligence, such as reversibility, allowed a whole set of syntactic structures to become accessible to learning.

One interesting finding was that intensive exposure to French facilitated the comprehension of certain English syntactic structures. This finding, together with the findings for the operational thought factor, were taken as support for the theory that a very similar deep structure underlies languages, and support for the hypothesis that learning processes similar to equilibration were operating in the acquisition of syntax.

In a detailed analysis of the pattern of errors, it was found that both English and French syntactic structures were acquired in approximately the same order and at about the same rate by children defined as 'balanced bilinguals'. These results replicated Kessler's major finding. When English syntactic

57

structures were sequenced by difficulty, the sequence generally replicated Kessler's findings, both when the performance of balanced bilinguals and the total sample was considered. The performance of children whose French was the weaker language accounted for deviations between the English and French sequences for the total sample.

The results of this study, therefore, supported Kessler's conclusion that certain aspects of the two languages of the bilingual child are not encoded separately when it comes to syntactic comprehension. It could be added that aspects of operational intelligence are not encoded separately from universal deep structure, and that this close relationship of syntactic and cognitive development becomes observable when syntax is defined in terms of Fillmore's case grammar.

Perhaps the most important results of this study are not in the answers, but in the questions it raises. Further research is needed to investigate the following problems:

(1) Whether syntax is acquired by means of equilibration principles.

(2) Whether intensive exposure to a second language can benefit operational intelligence in the transition period to the stage of concrete operations.

(3) How semantic feature development is related to performance on Piagetian tasks in pre-operational children.

(4) Which aspects of operational intelligence are most closely related to syntactic development. For example, it was not possible to assess how closely the seriation and conservation of volume tasks were related to syntactic comprehension because of the age range of subjects sampled.

(5) The relative contribution of various abilities for the auditory comprehension of synonymity both within and across languages in children whose second language is weaker than the first.

APPENDIX A

A SUMMARY OF CASE GRAMMAR THEORY

1.0 Case grammar in historical context. The model of case grammar used
in this study and in the Kessler (1971) study was first proposed by Fillmore
(1968, 1971), with certain modifications by Di Pietro (1971). This appendix
presents a simplified exposition of case grammar together with brief defini-
tions of terms and symbolic notation for the reader not familiar with recent
developments in linguistic theory.

Perhaps the simplest way to understand the basic notions of case grammar
is to relate them to the problems the theory was trying to resolve, in other
words, to contrast them with previous solutions. Fillmore's theory contrasts
both with the classical grammar tradition in which cases were defined as in-
flected forms of noun roots, such as the accusative, genitive, dative, etc.,
and with the recent transformational-generative (TG) grammar (Chomsky
1957, 1964), which did not use the notion of case at all. Fillmore resurrected
the idea of case for linguistic description, not to return to the traditional case
system, but to break through some impasses reached by TG grammar. His
theory rests on many assumptions of TG grammar, including the view that
'where our ancestors went wrong was in confusing what was "to be explained"
with what ought to be taken as "given".'

1.1 Deep structure and surface structure. These two concepts, originated
by Chomsky, are at the root of Fillmore's theory and must be understood if the
novelty of the theory is to be appreciated.

Following Chomsky, the surface structure of a sentence can be defined
loosely as the structural description of a sentence as it is actually said or
written. Surface structure often does not exhibit the underlying grammatical
relations which a person somehow infers in understanding the meaning of a
sentence.

Chomsky therefore hypothesized another level of structure which is 'covert'.
Deep structure can be loosely defined as the structural representation of what
a speaker-hearer must know to understand the sentences of his language.

To use the classical examples, although 'John is eager to please' and
'John is easy to please' appear to be structurally identical, Chomsky (1957)
showed that to understand the two sentences, a person must perceive the
underlying grammatical relations (deep structure) which are not identical
for the two cases, as represented in Figure A1.

FIGURE A1.

[(subj.) pleases John]   [It is easy]
[John pleases (obj.)]   [John is eager]

Fillmore recognized the need for the deep-surface structure distinction in linguistic theory, but he proposed an alternative way of thinking about and representing 'covert categories', a way which suggested solutions for certain contradictions which ensued from defining deep structure independently of semantics, as Chomsky had done.

2.0 The case structure of sentences. In TG grammar, case inflections were viewed as a phenomenon of the surface structure. Fillmore argued that cases must be an integral part of the deep structure of all languages, realized in surface structure sometimes as inflections, sometimes as prepositions or word order, and defined as abstract relations between sentence components.

2.1 The set of case categories. Although Fillmore tried to avoid defining the cases in terms of the semantic function of sentence parts in the surface structure, he was not entirely successful. The deep structure of simple sentences was said to 'identify the underlying syntactic-semantic relationship' between a verb (V) and an unordered array of noun phrases (NP) which hold special labelled relations (cases) to the sentence or proposition (SENT). 'Case notions comprise a set of universal, presumably innate, concepts which identify certain types of judgments human beings are capable of making about the events that are going on around them, judgments about such matters as who did it, who it happened to, and what got changed' (1968:24). How the set of cases are to be limited in number and how they can be identified from surface structure remains controversial and constitutes the weakest part of the theory.

The set of case categories with which this study was concerned is agentive (A), objective (O), source (S), goal (G), and benefactive (B). The basic deep structure of language from which surface structures are realized can therefore be represented by a tree diagram, as in Figure A2.

FIGURE A2

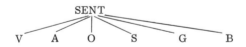

SENT

V   A   O   S   G   B

2.2 Case frame notation. Once a particular verb is selected, SENT can be represented as a set of cases specifying the verb. For example, the case frame for the surface structure active can be represented as V[__AO]. That is, the active verb is defined by its relationship to the agentive and objective cases.

2.3 Simple and embedded sentences. In simple sentences, the verb is inserted in the case frame V[__AOSG(B)], where all but the benefactive case must be accounted for. Embedded sentences are noun phrases in the deep structure of a simple sentence which have been expanded into a sentence. An embedded sentence, therefore, takes on the characteristics of the case role from which it was expanded. See Appendix C for a list and description of the simple and embedded sentences tested in this study.

2.4 Co-referential cases. In order to account for all the case roles which define simple sentences, the surface reflexive structure (i. e. 'the girls see themselves') is represented by the case frame V[__AOSG]/A=OSG, where the agentive is co-referential with objective, source, and goal. That is, A has the same logical referent as O, S, and G. The theory would suggest that the listener learns to distinguish between the reflexive and the reciprocal (i. e. 'the girls see themselves'/'the girls see each other') by learning which cases are co-referential. Contrasted with the reflexive, the verb of the reciprocal structure fits into the case frame V[__AOSG]/A=SG, with a pronoun selected from a particular set for the O case.

2.5 Subject and object selection hierarchy. A definable hierarchy can be specified for the selection of the surface subject and object manifestations from the set of deep structure cases. That is, the particular case in a sentence which outranks the others will have the noun phrase associated with it selected as the surface subject. The normal subject selection hierarchy is given by A-O-S-G, which states that A, if present, is selected as subject in preference to the other cases. If A is not present, O is selected in preference to the other cases, and so on. The object hierarchy is O-G.

2.6 Rank-shift. When the surface structure of a sentence requires a shift in the rank order of the subject or object hierarchy, that sentence will be more difficult to comprehend than a sentence with the normal rank order. For example, both the surface active and passive structures have the case frame V[__AO], but the passive requires that the O become the surface subject. Therefore the passive should be more difficult to comprehend than the active.

Similarly, verbs which take the for-to construction fit into the case frame V[__AOSG(B)]/A=S. That is, the A and S cases are co-referential and the B case is optional. This case frame is identical to the one which takes the to-for construction. For-to, therefore, should be more difficult to comprehend than to-for because a rank shift has occurred in the normal order of the G and B cases.

Another structure tested in the study which required a rank-shift was the direct/indirect object inversion, which fits into the case frame V[__AOSG]/A=S. In the sentence 'the boy shows the bird the cat', therefore, a rank shift has occurred between the O and G cases. (See Appendix C, p. 71, for test items manifesting rank-shift.)

3.0 Syntactic features. Some universal grammatical categories can be further specified in terms of syntactic features. For example, noun phrases may be marked [+ pronoun] to indicate pronoun suitability for the noun, or verbs may be marked [+ adjective] to represent surface realizations as an adjective. The group of inflectional categories tested in this study and in the Kessler (1971) study was described in terms of syntactic features (see Appendix C, p. 70).

TESTING AND SCORING PROCEDURE
FOR THE PIAGETIAN TESTS

1. Seriation

Testing procedure

1. Demonstrate seriation of the staircase using the first set of 10 slats, while saying, 'Watch what I'm going to do. I'm making a staircase'. Then break up the staircase and say, 'Now you make a staircase just like I did, just like mine'. If child correctly seriates 10 slats, go to item 8 below.
ANSWER: RIGHT_____
                                              WRONG_____

2. If child unable to seriate the 10 slats, remove the 5 smallest and let him seriate these, saying, 'Now see if you can make me a staircase'.
ANSWER: RIGHT_____
                                                WRONG_____

3. If child cannot seriate 5, discontinue experiment.

4. If child correctly seriates 5, break up the staircase and give him 7 slats to seriate.
ANSWER: RIGHT_____
                                              WRONG_____

5. If child cannot seriate 7, discontinue experiment.

6. If child correctly seriates 7, break up staircase and give him 10 slats to seriate.
ANSWER: RIGHT_____
                                              WRONG_____

7. If child cannot seriate 10 slats, discontinue experiment.

8. If child correctly seriates 10 slats, produce the second set of 9 slats, saying, 'Can you put these slats in their right places in the staircase? Can you put

them where they fit in the staircase to make a longer staircase?'. If child does not understand that the new slats should be put in between the original ones, prompt once: 'Make one big long staircase, put the new stairs in between the old staircase. . . . Pretend these were left out when you made the short staircase, and now you have to fit them in their right places'.

ANSWER: RIGHT_____
WRONG_____

Scoring procedure

Method 1. The child is awarded points according to the following criteria, and the points are added up to obtain the Seriation Score.
1 - seriates 5
1 - seriates 7
1 - seriates 10
3 - seriates second set of 9 correctly

Method 2. The child is classified as non-operational if he is unable to seriate, or if he forms very small series with the slats, or forms a series but ignores the base of the slats thereby creating an uneven seriation, or if the child forms the first seriation by trial and error, taking a long time, and cannot insert the second series.
The child is classified as operational if he correctly seriates both sets of slats.

2. Numeration

Testing procedure

1. Place the correctly seriated first set of 10 slats before the child and produce the farmer, a small plastic figure of a man carrying a little lamb. Place the farmer on the ground and make him climb to the first stair, asking, 'If the farmer starts on the ground, how many stairs does he have to climb to reach this stair?'. Place the farmer on the second stair and ask the same question--continue to the tenth stair.

RIGHT_____
WRONG_____

2. 'How many stairs does he have to climb to reach this stair?' (4)

RIGHT_____
OTHER_____

3. 'How many stairs does he have to climb to reach this stair?' (7)

RIGHT_____
OTHER_____

4. Break up the staircase so that the slats are disarranged on the table. Point to the second stair. 'How many stairs does he have to climb to reach this stair, if the staircase was together like it was before?' 'How do you know?'

RIGHT_____   Reseriates to 2_____
OTHER_____   Reseriates beyond 2_____
                                 Answers without
                                 reseriating_____

WHY?

5. If child answers wrong from memory, suggest reconstructing the staircase:
'How would you find the answer? How would you make sure of your answer?'
'Try putting the staircase together again'. After the child has answered, say,
'How do you know?'
RIGHT_____   Reseriates to 2_____
OTHER_____   Reseriates beyond 2_____
                                 Doesn't reseriate_____
WHY?

6. Break up the staircase if need be. 'How many stairs does he have to
climb to reach the top, if he was standing on this stair?' (2) 'How do you
know?'
RIGHT_____   Subtracts mentally_____
OTHER_____   Appears to count the dis-
                                 arranged slats_____
                                 Seriates again and appears
                                 to count_____
WHY?

7. Break up the staircase if need be. Point to the fifth stair. 'How many
stairs does he have to climb to reach this stair, if the staircase was together
like it was before?' 'How do you know?'
RIGHT_____   Reseriates to 5_____
OTHER_____   Reseriates beyond 5_____
                                 Answers without
                                 reseriating_____
WHY?

8. If child answers wrong from memory, suggest reconstructing the stair-
case as in item 5 above.
RIGHT_____   Reseriates to 5_____
OTHER_____   Reseriates beyond 5_____
                                 Doesn't reseriate_____
WHY?

9. Break up the staircase if need be. 'How many stairs does he have to
climb to reach the top, if he was standing on this stair?' (5) 'How do you
know?'
RIGHT_____   Subtracts mentally_____
WRONG_____   Appears to count the dis-
                                 arranged slats_____
                                 Seriates again and appears
                                 to count_____
WHY?

Scoring Procedure

Method 1. The child is awarded points according to the following criteria, and the points are added up to obtain the Numeration score.

1 - gets the idea in item 1 and counts all ten slats correctly
1 - answers correctly to items 2 and 3, or answers minus one of the right answer in both cases
1 - answers correctly on item 4 or item 5 without reseriating, or reseriates to the second slat only
1 - answers correctly on item 6, appears to subtract mentally, and offers appropriate explanation (i. e. 'Because two and eight is ten')
1 - answers correctly on item 7 or 8 without reseriating, or reseriates to the fifth slat only
1 - answers correctly on item 9, appears to subtract mentally, and offers appropriate explanation

Method 2. The child is classified as non-operational if he shows any or all of the following behaviors:

(a) he is unable to grasp the problem of the number of stairs the farmer has climbed, unable to get the idea that the number of stairs climbed is determined by the number of the stair.
(b) he is able to grasp the initial counting of the number of stairs, although he may think that to reach stair four, three stairs have been climbed.
(c) he has problems with counting when the stairs are disarranged, and may not realize that the number of stairs left to climb is determined by the number of stairs already climbed, so that he has to reconstruct the whole series.

The child is classified as operational if he answers correctly when questioned about the arranged and disarranged series, and realizes that he does not have to reconstruct the whole series in order to determine how many stairs are left to climb after a certain stair has been reached.

3. Conservation of mass

Testing procedure

1. Produce four Play-Doh balls, two the same size and all of different colors. 'Choose two that have the same amount of Play-Doh, that are the same size.' If child replies that they are all different, say, 'True, in color they are different, but I'm thinking of amount of Play-Doh. Which two are the same?' Discontinue experiment if the child cannot choose the correct two.

2. Take the two balls which were chosen, and put away the other two. 'Is there as much Play-Doh in this ball as in that one?', while pointing to the two balls of equal size. If the child does not agree, discontinue the experiment.

3.* 'Now watch what I do.' Roll one of the balls into a sausage.
'Is there the same amount of Play-Doh in the sausage as in the ball?'
'How can you tell?'
    YES_____   NO_____   WHY?

4.* 'Does one have more Play-Doh?' If the child answers yes, say, 'Which
one?' 'How can you tell?'
    YES_____   NO_____   WHY?   WHICH ONE?_____

5.* Roll the sausage some more, making it very long and skinny. 'Is there
the same amount of Play-Doh in the sausage as in the ball now?' 'How can
you tell?'
    YES_____   NO_____   WHY?

6.* 'Does one have more Play-Doh?' If the child answers yes, say, 'Which
one?' 'How can you tell?'
    YES_____   NO_____   WHY?   WHICH ONE?_____

7.* Break the sausage into three pieces. 'Is there the same amount of
Play-Doh in the ball as in the three pieces?' 'How can you tell?'
    YES_____   NO_____   WHY?

8.* 'Does this have more now, or does this have more?' indicating the ball
and the three pieces.' 'Which one?' 'How can you tell?'
    YES_____   NO_____   WHY?   WHICH ONE?_____

Scoring procedure

Method 1. The child is awarded one point if he answers correctly on each
of items 3, 4, 5, 6, 7, and 8, and if he gives an appropriate explanation for
each question. Explanations were considered indicative of conservation
according to the criteria outlined in Elkind (1961) and Brainerd (1971).

Method 2. The child is classified as non-operational if he shows any or
all of the following behaviors:

(a) he cannot choose the two equal balls.
(b) he does not admit equality after having chosen them.
(c) after having chosen the two balls and having admitted equality, he
    gives conservation answers to some, but not all of the questions
    and offers at least one non-conserving explanation.

The child is classified as operational if he consistently gives conservation
answers and explanations.

_____

*The order of presenting the two questions for each transformation was
counterbalanced. That is, half the subjects in each grade and each curriculum were asked questions 3, 5, and 7 first, while the other half were
asked questions 4, 6, and 8 first.

4. Conservation of weight

Testing procedure

1. Produce four Play-Doh balls, two the same size and all of different colors. 'Choose the two that weigh the same, the two which have the same amount of weight.' If the child cannot choose them, say, 'Can you make two the same weight?' If the child cannot agree, even after handling the balls and taking pieces off one or the other, that two weigh the same, discontinue the experiment.

2. Take the two balls which were chosen, and put away the other two. 'Does this ball weigh the same as this one?' 'Do they have the same amount of weight?' If the child does not agree, discontinue the experiment.

3. * 'Now watch what I do.' Flatten one ball into a pancake.
   'Does the ball weigh the same amount as the pancake?'
   'How can you tell?'
   YES_____   NO_____   WHY?

4. * 'Does one weigh more?' If the child answers yes, say, 'Which one?'
   'How can you tell?'
   YES_____   NO_____   WHY?   WHICH ONE?_____

5. * Flatten the pancake some more, making it very thin and spreading it over a large area. 'Are they the same weight now?' 'How can you tell?'
   YES_____   NO_____   WHY?

6. * 'Does one weigh more now?' If the child answers yes, say, 'Which one?' 'How can you tell?'
   YES_____   NO_____   WHY?   WHICH ONE?_____

7. * Break the pancake into three pieces. 'Does the ball weigh the same amount as these three pieces?' 'How can you tell?'
   YES_____   NO_____   WHY?

8. * 'Does this weigh more now, or does this weigh more?' indicating the ball and the three pieces. 'Which one?' 'How can you tell?'
   YES_____   NO_____   WHY?   WHICH ONE?_____

Scoring procedure

Method 1. The child is awarded one point if he answers correctly on each of items 3, 4, 5, 6, 7, and 8 and if he gives an appropriate explanation for each question.

Method 2. The criteria for classifying subjects as operational or non-operational were the same as for the conservation of mass task.

_____

*The order of presenting the two questions for each transformation was counterbalanced, as in the conservation of mass task.

5. Conservation of volume

Testing procedure

1. Produce the beaker two-thirds full of water with a rubber band around it. Place a ball of plasticene in the water, drawing the child's attention to what is happening. 'Let's put the rubber band to where the water goes up.' Encourage the child to do this.

2. After the water level has been marked, remove the ball from the water slowly, saying, 'Watch what's happening to the water.' Dry the ball with a paper towel and flatten it into a pancake.

3.* 'If I place the pancake in the beaker, will the water go <u>below</u> the rubber band?' 'Why?'
YES_____ NO_____ WHY?

4.* 'If I place the pancake in the beaker, will the water go <u>right back</u> to the rubber band?' 'Why?'
YES_____ NO_____ WHY?

5.* 'If I place the pancake in the beaker, will the water go <u>above</u> the rubber band?' 'Why?'
YES_____ NO_____ WHY?

(If the child is not giving many responses for his judgments, encourage him, saying, 'Tell me more, etc.' Each of the three questions are asked separately and subsequent questions are not asked until the previous ones are answered.)

6. Place the pancake in the water and let the child observe what happens. Take it out and dry it off again. Tear the pancake into three pieces. 'If I place these three pieces in the beaker, where do you think the water will go up to?' Encourage the child to show you with his finger. 'How can you tell?'
TO THE RUBBER BAND_____
BELOW THE RUBBER BAND_____
ABOVE THE RUBBER BAND_____ WHY?

7. Place the three pieces in the water, being careful not to let any plasticene stick above the water, and let the child observe. Take them out again, dry them off, and roll them into a pillar shape, long enough so that it will stick above water level. 'If I place this pillar in the beaker so that it stands up, where will the water go up to?' Encourage the child to show you with his finger. 'How can you tell?'
TO THE RUBBER BAND_____
BELOW THE RUBBER BAND_____
ABOVE THE RUBBER BAND_____ WHY?

---

*The order of presenting items 3, 4, and 5 was random.

Scoring procedure

Method 1. The child is awarded one point if he answers correctly on each of items 3, 4, 5, and 6 and if he offers appropriate explanations for each question. He is awarded one point for answering question 7 correctly, and one point if he offers an adequate explanation for question 7.

Method 2. The child is classified as non-operational if he is not consistently correct in his answers and explanations, and operational if he is consistently correct.

SYNTACTIC CONTRASTS TESTED IN THE STUDY

1. Inflectional categories

The few inflectional categories Kessler chose for testing were those which she felt might provide information for interpreting the sequencing of other syntactic structures. Six different combinations of word class categories with associated feature specifications were tested.

English	French

1. Verb tense (V[+present, +past])

he buys a ticket	il achète un billet
he bought a ticket	il a acheté un billet
he will buy a ticket	il va acheter un billet
he is eating	il mange
he ate	il a mangé
he will eat	il va manger

2. Pronoun object – gender (direct only – indirect has no gender distinction in French) (P[+masculine])

she sees him	elle le voit
she sees her	elle la voit
he pushes her	il la pousse
he pushes him	il le pousse

3. Verb person – number (V[+3 singular])

he writes	il écrit
they write	ils écrivent
he opens the window	il ouvre la fenêtre
they open the window	ils ouvrent la fenêtre

4. Possessive adjective - number (Adj[+3 singular])

his ball	sa balle
their ball	leur balle
his dog	son chien
their dog	leur chien

5. Noun gender (N[+masculine])

the boy	le garçon
the girl	la fille
the grandfather	le grand-père
the grandmother	la grand-mère

6. Noun number (N[+singular])

the book	le livre
the books	les livres
the dog	le chien
the dogs	les chiens

2. Syntactic structures

The eleven syntactic structures tested can be divided into two types--those involving case relations in simple sentences and those involving embedding of one sentence within another.

Case relations in simple sentences. In this set of contrasts, the verb is specified in terms of five cases: agentive (A), objective (0), source (S), goal (G), and benefactive (B). In case frame notation, the verb is inserted in V[__AOSG(B)], where all but the benefactive case must be accounted for. The case relations tested were A-O, A-G, O-G, S-G, and G-B. In case grammar theory, a definable hierarchy can be specified for the selection of surface subject and object manifestations from the set of deep structure cases. When the normal ordering of cases is violated, as in contrasts 2, 5a, and 7 below, complexity can be expected to increase. Similarly, complexity increases when verbs fitting into the same case frame differ in the co-referentiality of the noun phrases (NP's), as in contrast 3 below.

English

1. Active (A-O)

the baby sees the girl
the girl sees the baby

the boy hits the ball
the ball hits the boy

2. Passive (O-A)

    the girl is seen by the baby
    the baby is seen by the girl

    the ball is hit by the boy
    the boy is hit by the ball

3. Reflexive/reciprocal (A-O) - reflexive V[__AOSG]/A = OSG
                                  reciprocal V[__AOSG]/A = SG

    the boys see themselves
    the boys see each other

    the girls see themselves
    the girls see each other

4. Subject/indirect object (A-G)

    the baby gives the ball to the girl
    the girl gives the ball to the baby

    the boy brings the dog to the mother
    the mother brings the dog to the boy

5. Direct/indirect object (O-G)

    the girl shows the cow to the dog
    the girl shows the dog to the cow

    the boy brings the mouse to the cat
    the boy brings the cat to the mouse

5a. English-specific direct/indirect object inversion (G-O)
    SOME SUBJECTS ONLY

    the boy shows the cat the bird
    the boy shows the bird the cat

6. From-to (S-G)

    the baby goes from the window to the door
    the baby goes from the door to the window

    the cat jumps from the table to the floor
    the cat jumps from the floor to the table

7. For-to (B-G)

    the baby gives the ball for the cat to the dog
    the baby gives the ball for the dog to the cat

the girl brings the ball for the baby to the mother
the girl brings the ball for the mother to the baby

French

1. Active (A-O)

   le bébé voit la fille
   la fille voit le bébé

   le garçon frappe la balle
   la balle frappe le garçon

2. Passive (O-A)

   la fille est vue par le bébé
   le bébé est vu par la fille

   la balle est frappée par le garçon
   le garçon est frappé par la balle

3. Reflexive/reciprocal (A-O) - reflexive V[__AOSG]/A = OSG
   reciprocal V[__AOSG]/A = SG

   les garçons se regardent
   les garçons se regardent les uns les autres

   les filles se regardent
   les filles se regardent les unes les autres

4. Subject/indirect object (A-G)

   le bébé donne la balle à la fille
   la fille donne la balle au bébé

   le garçon apporte le chien à la mère
   la mère apporte le chien au garçon

5. Direct/indirect object (O-G)

   la fille montre la vache au chien
   la fille montre le chien à la vache

   le garçon apporte la souris au chat
   le garçon apporte le chat à la souris

6. From-to (S-G)

   le bébé va de la fenêtre à la porte
   le bébé va de la porte à la fenêtre

le chat saute de la table au plancher
le chat saute du plancher à la table

7. For-to (B-G)

le bébé donne la balle pour le chat au chien
le bébé donne la balle pour le chien au chat

la fille apporte la balle pour le bébé à la mère
la fille apporte la balle pour la mère au bébé

7a. French only - to-for (G-B)   SOME SUBJECTS ONLY

la mère montre le livre à la fille pour le garçon
la mère montre le livre au garçon pour la fille

Embeddings

Three types of embedding (noun phrases in deep structure expanded to include a sentence--N-SENT) were tested: embedded sentences whose verbs are specified with a [± adjective] feature; embedded sentences whose verbs are represented by the case frame V[__OL]; and embedded sentences whose verbs are represented by the case frame V[__OG].

English

8. Noun/adjective (N-SENT: V[+adj]) - single embedding

the dog with a big ball
the big dog with a ball

the cat with a big bird
the big cat with a bird

9. Comparative adjective (N-SENT: V[+adj]) - multiple embedding

the car is longer than the truck
the truck is longer than the car

the black ball is larger than the white one
the white ball is larger than the black one

10. Relative clause (N-SENT: V[__OL]) - embedded under A or O in matrix sentence

the baby on the table eats the cake
the baby eats the cake which is on the table

the cat on the chair scares the bird
the cat scares the bird which is on the chair

11. Possessive x of y (N-SENT: V[__OG])

    the plane of the pilot
    the pilot of the plane

    the king of the castle
    the castle of the king

French

8. Noun/adjective (N-SENT: V[+adj]) - single embedding

    le chien avec une grosse balle
    le gros chien avec une balle

    le chat avec un gros oiseau
    le gros chat avec un oiseau

9. Comparative adjective (N-SENT: V[+adj]) - multiple embedding

    la voiture est plus longue que le camion
    le camion est plus long que la voiture

    la balle noire est plus grosse que la blanche
    la balle blanche est plus grosse que la noire

10. Relative clause (N-SENT: V[__OL]) - embedded under A or O in matrix sentence

    le bébé sur la table mange du gâteau
    le bébé mange le gâteau qui est sur la table

    le chat sur la chaise fait peur à l'oiseau
    le chat fait peur à l'oiseau qui est sur la chaise

11. Possessive x of y (N-SENT: V[__OG])

    le pilote de l'avion
    l'avion du pilote

    le roi du château
    le château du roi

3. Synonymous sentences within languages (English)

1. Active/passive (A-O/O-A)

    the truck pushes the car
    (a) the car is pushed by the truck
    (b) the truck is pushed by the car

the boy hits the ball
(a) the ball is hit by the boy
(b) the boy is hit by the ball

2. Passive/active (O-A/A-O)

the boy is hit by the ball
(a) the boy hits the ball
(b) the ball hits the boy

the car is pushed by the truck
(a) the truck pushes the car
(b) the car pushes the truck

3. Relative clause/adjective (N-SENT: V[+adj]/N-adj)

the ball which is white is near the dog
(a) the white ball is near the dog
(b) the ball is near the white dog

the cat has a ball which is black
(a) the black cat has a ball
(b) the cat has a black ball

4. Possessive noun phrase/noun phrase (N-SENT: NP:G[+adj]/NP)

I see the castle of the king
(a) I see the castle
(b) I see the king

I see the pilot of the plane
(a) I see the plane
(b) I see the pilot

5. Noun phrase/object pronoun (direct) (NP-O[+pro]/Pro)

The boy pushes the girl
(a) the boy pushes him
(b) the boy pushes her

the boy sees the flower
(a) the boy sees her
(b) the boy sees it

4. Synonymous sentences within languages (French)

1. Active/passive (A-O/O-A)

le camion pousse la voiture
(a) la voiture est poussée par le camion
(b) le camion est poussé par la voiture

le garçon frappe la balle
(a) la balle est frappée par le garçon
(b) le garçon est frappé par la balle

2. Passive/active (O-A/A-O)

le garçon est frappé par la balle
(a) le garçon frappe la balle
(b) la balle frappe le garçon

la voiture est poussée par le camion
(a) le camion pousse la voiture
(b) la voiture pousse le camion

3. Relative clause/adjective (N-SENT: V[+adj]/N-adj)

la balle qui est blanche est près du chien
(a) la balle blanche est près du chien
(b) la balle est près du chien blanc

le chat a une balle qui est noire
(a) le chat noir a une balle
(b) le chat a une balle noire

4. Possessive noun phrase/noun phrase (N-SENT: NP:G[+adj]/NP)

Je vois le pilote de l'avion
(a) je vois le pilote
(b) je vois l'avion

Je vois le château du roi
(a) je vois le roi
(b) je vois le château

5. Noun phrase/object pronoun (direct) (NP-O[+pro]/Pro)

le garçon pousse la fille
(a) le garçon le pousse
(b) le garçon la pousse

le garçon regarde la fleur
(a) la garçon le regarde
(b) le garçon la regarde

5. Across-languages test

Similar structures

1. Relative clause (N-SENT)

the car which is big pushes the truck
(a) la voiture qui est grande pousse le camion
(b) la voiture pousse le camion qui est grand

le chat a une balle qui est noire
(a) the cat has a ball which is black
(b) the cat which is black has a ball

2. Subject pronoun (NP-A[+pro])

la mère dit qu'il est dans la cuisine
(a) the mother says she is in the kitchen
(b) the mother says he is in the kitchen

the mother says he is coming
(a) la mère dit qu'il vient
(b) la mère dit qu'elle vient

3. Object pronoun (NP-O[+pro])

le garçon la pousse
(a) the boy pushes him
(b) the boy pushes her

the girl sees him
(a) la fille le voit
(b) la fille la voit

4. Active/passive (A-O/O-A)

le bébé voit la mère
(a) the mother sees the baby
(b) the baby sees the mother

the mother is seen by the baby
(a) le bébé est vu par la mère
(b) la mère est vue par le bébé

Syntactic variants

1. Active/passive (A-O/O-A)

the car pushes the truck
(a) la voiture est poussée par le camion
(b) le camion est poussé par la voiture

la balle frappe le garçon
(a) the ball is hit by the boy
(b) the boy is hit by the ball

2. Passive/active (O-A/A-O)

> the mother is seen by the baby
> (a) le bébé voit la mère
> (b) la mère voit le bébé
>
> la voiture est poussée par le camion
> (a) the truck pushes the car
> (b) the car pushes the truck

3. Relative clause/adjective (N-SENT: V[+adj]/N-Adj)

> the ball which is white is near the dog
> (a) la balle blanche est près du chien
> (b) la balle est près du chien blanc
>
> la voiture qui est longue pousse le camion
> (a) the car pushes the long truck
> (b) the long car pushes the truck

4. Possessive noun phrase/noun phrase (N-SENT: NP:G[+adj]/NP)

> I see the pilot of the plane
> (a) je vois le pilote
> (b) je vois l'avion
>
> je vois le roi du château
> (a) I see the castle
> (b) I see the king

5. Noun phrase/subject pronoun (NP-A[+pro]/Pro)

> the mother says the boy is coming
> (a) la mère dit qu'il vient
> (b) la mère dit qu'elle vient
>
> la mère dit que les garçons viennent
> (a) the mother says he is coming
> (b) the mother says they are coming

6. Noun phrase/object pronoun (NP-O[+pro]/Pro)

> the baby sees the girl
> (a) le bébé la voit
> (b) le bébé le voit
>
> le garçon pousse la fille
> (a) the boy pushes her
> (b) the boy pushes him

APPENDIX D

PICTURES USED FOR THE SYNTACTIC
COMPREHENSION TESTS

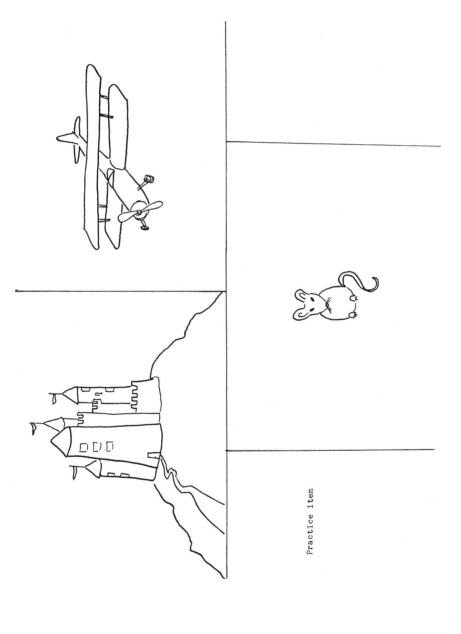

Practice item

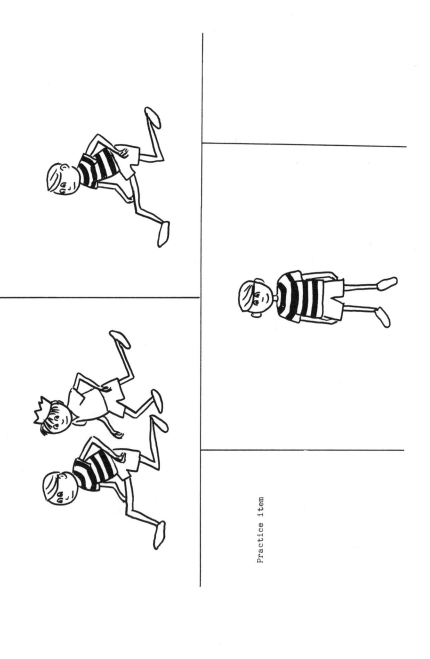

Practice item

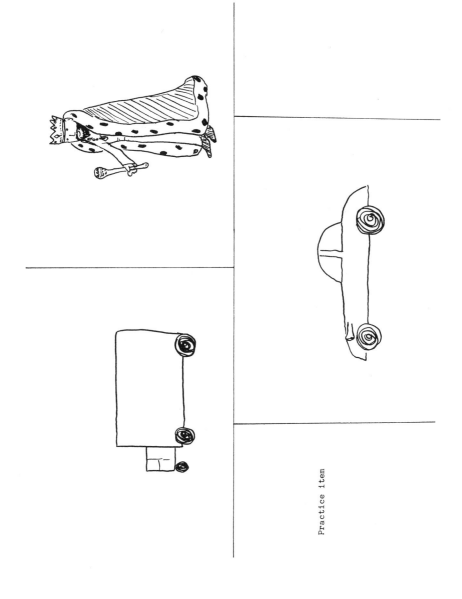

Practice item

Practice item

he buys a ticket/
he bought a ticket

he will buy a ticket/
he buys a ticket

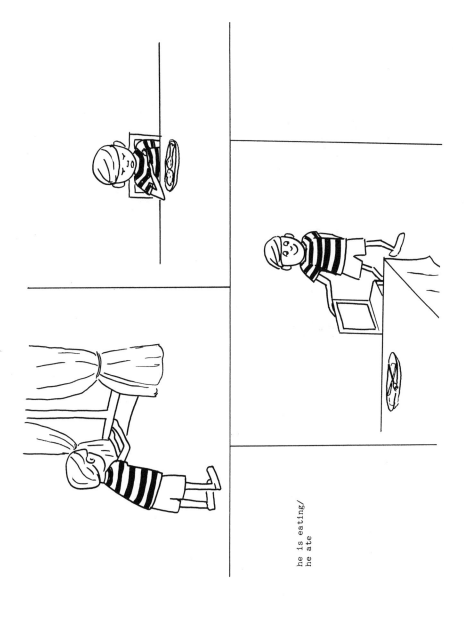

he is eating/
he ate

he will eat/
he is eating

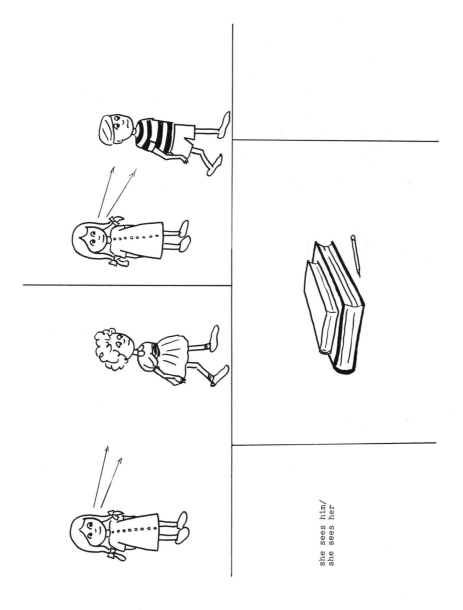

she sees him/
she sees her

he pushes her/
he pushes him

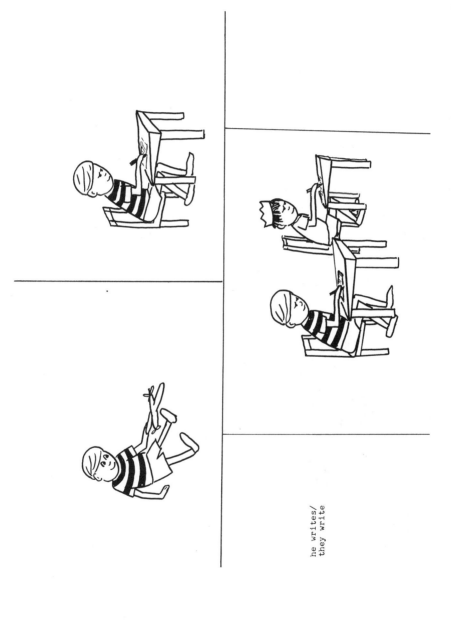

he writes/
they write

he opens the window/
they open the window

his ball/
their ball

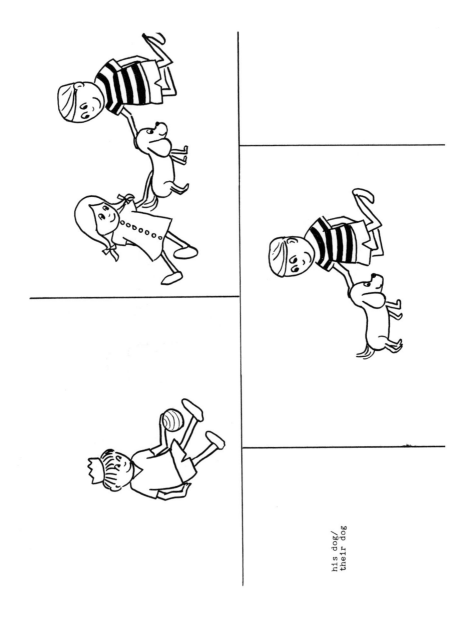

his dog/
their dog

the girl/
the boy

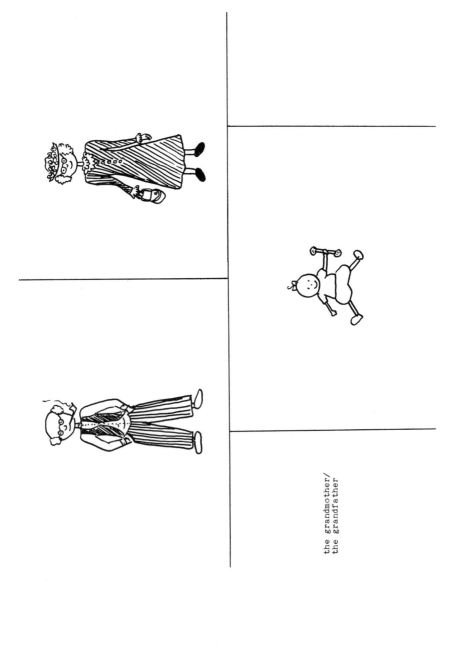

the grandmother/
the grandfather

the book/
the books

the dog/
the dogs

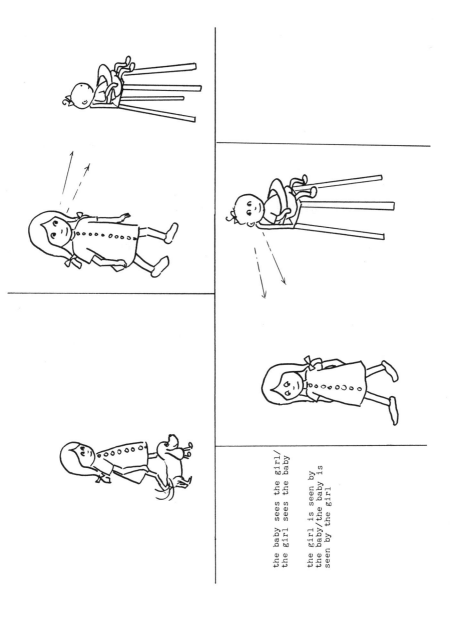

the baby sees the girl/
the girl sees the baby

the girl is seen by
the baby/the baby is
seen by the girl

the boy hits the ball/
the ball hits the boy

the boy is hit by the
ball/the ball is hit
by the boy

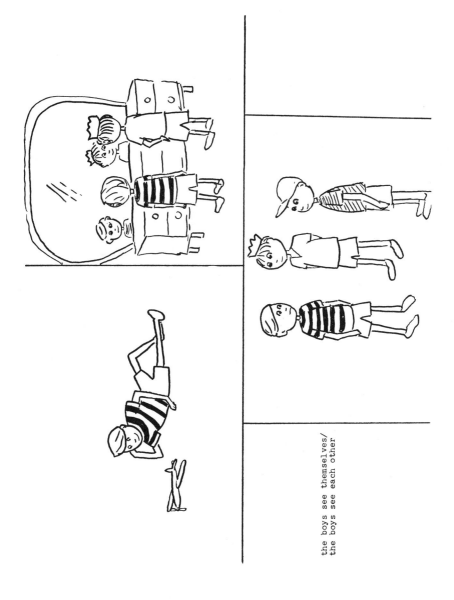

the boys see themselves/
the boys see each other

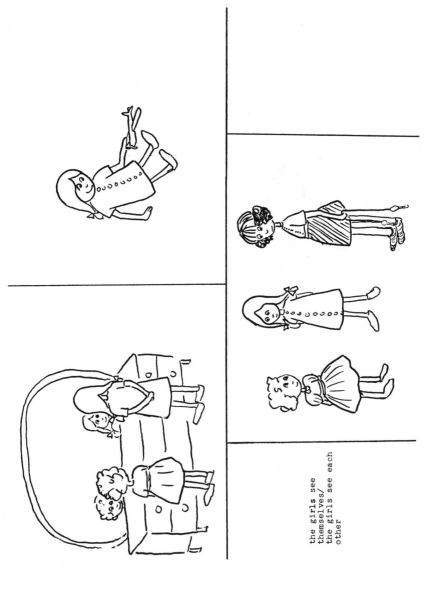

the girls see
themselves/
the girls see each
other

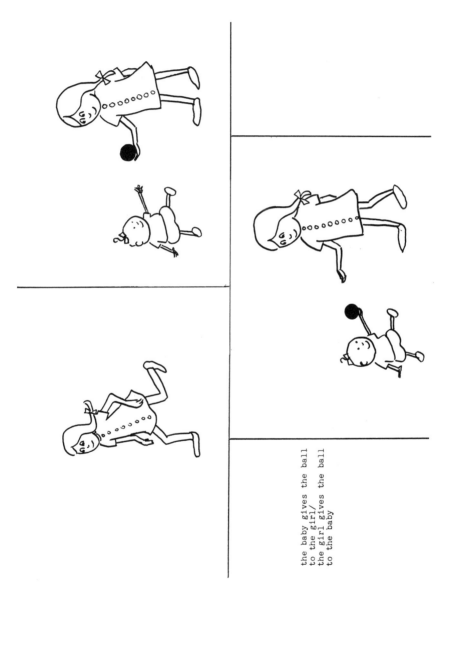

the baby gives the ball
to the girl/
the girl gives the ball
to the baby

the boy brings the dog
to the mother/
the mother brings the
dog to the boy

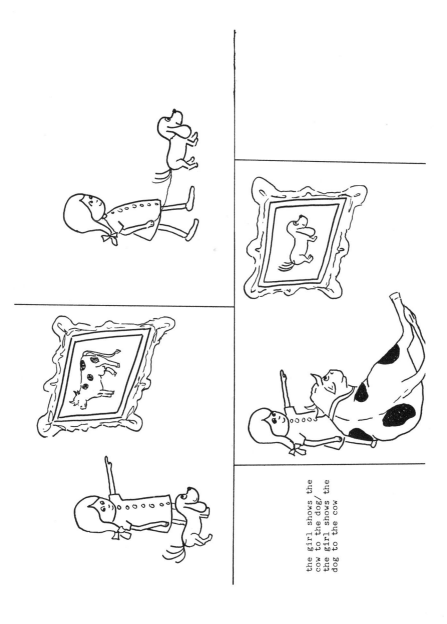

the girl shows the cow to the dog/ the girl shows the dog to the cow

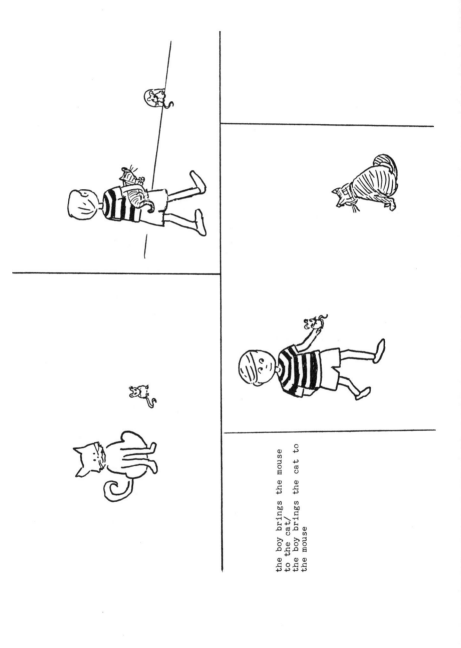

the boy brings the mouse
to the cat/
the boy brings the cat to
the mouse

Direct/indirect object
inversion

the boy shows the cat
the bird/the boy shows
the bird the cat

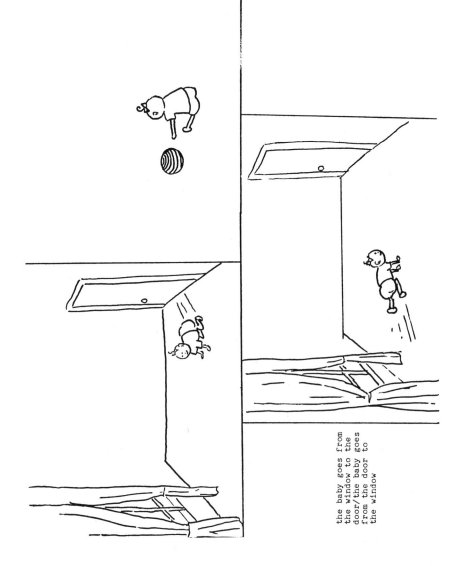

the baby goes from
the window to the
door/the baby goes
from the door to
the window

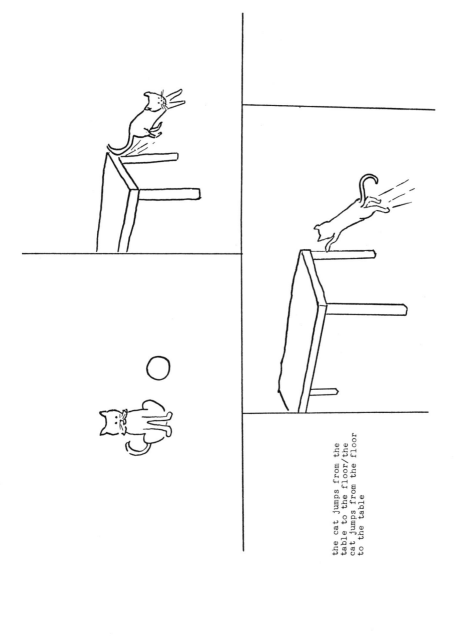

the cat jumps from the
table to the floor/the
cat jumps from the floor
to the table

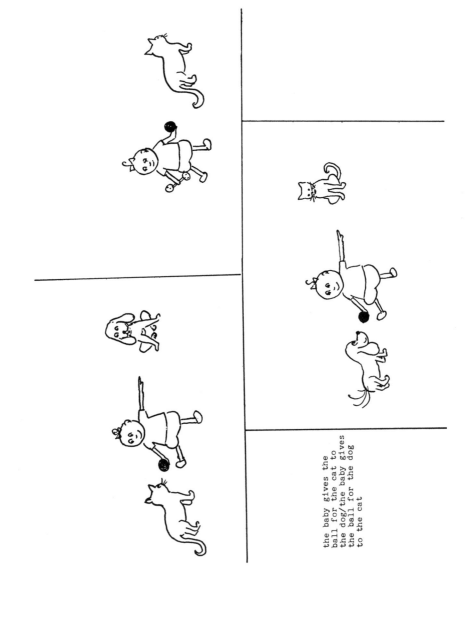

the baby gives the
ball for the cat to
the dog/the baby gives
the ball for the dog
to the cat

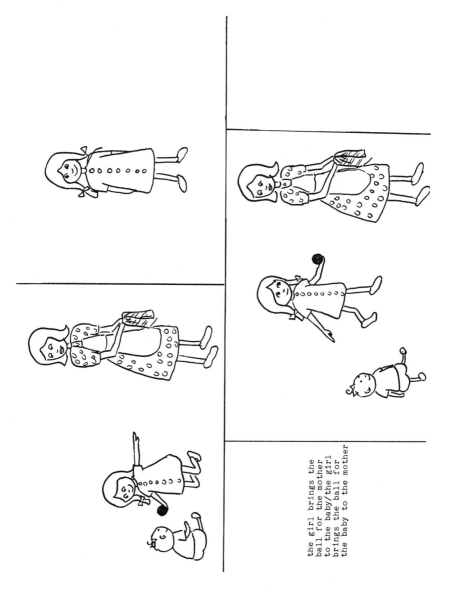

the girl brings the
ball for the mother
to the baby/the girl
brings the ball for
the baby to the mother

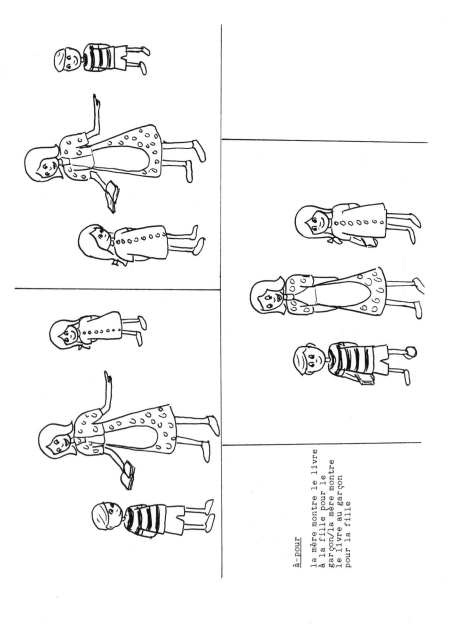

à-pour

la mère montre le livre
à la fille pour le
garçon/la mère montre
le livre au garçon
pour la fille

the dog with a big ball/
the big dog with a ball

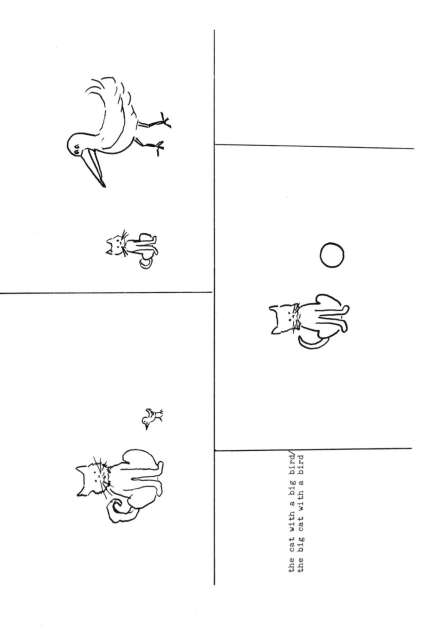

the cat with a big bird/
the big cat with a bird

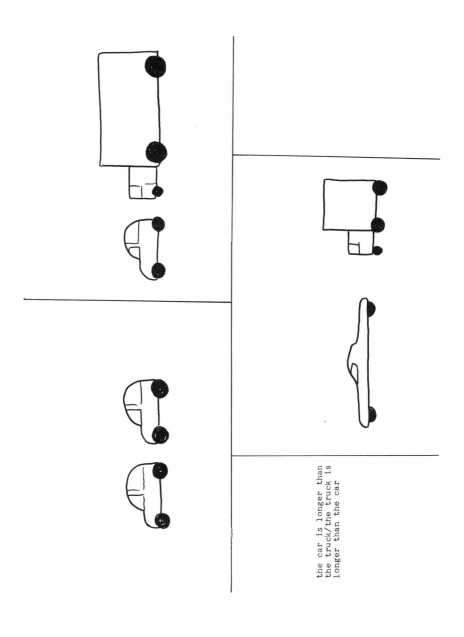

the car is longer than
the truck/the truck is
longer than the car

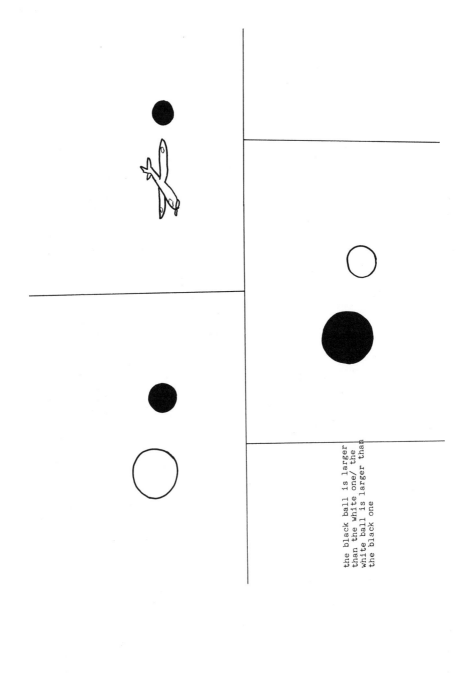

the black ball is larger
than the white one/ the
white ball is larger than
the black one

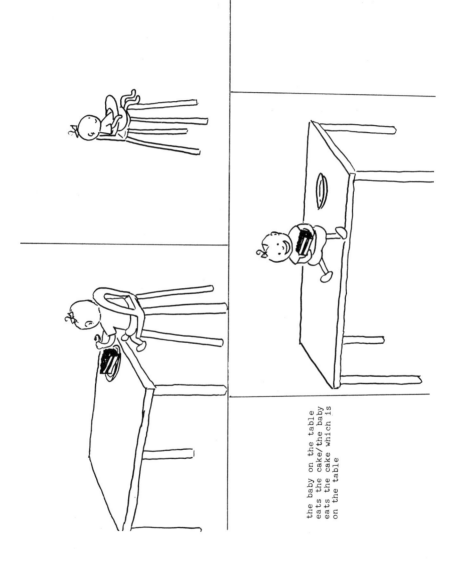

the baby on the table
eats the cake/the baby
eats the cake which is
on the table

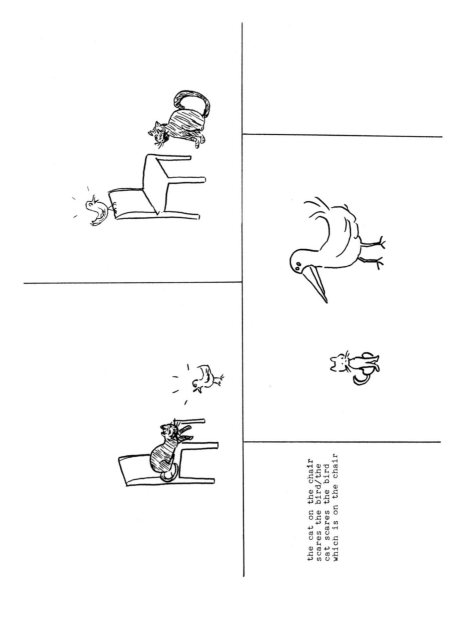

the cat on the chair
scares the bird/the
cat scares the bird
which is on the chair

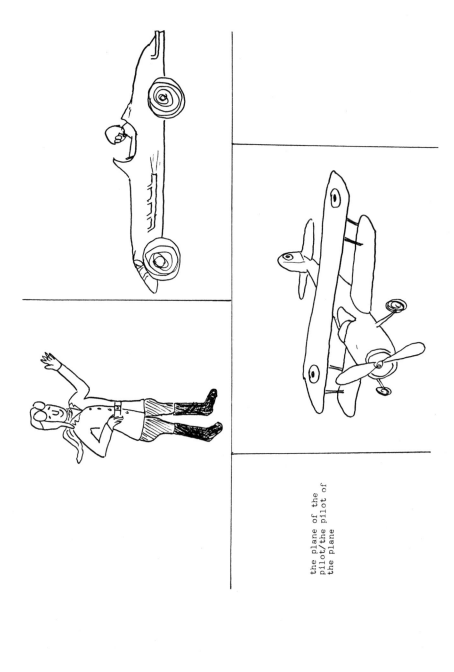

the plane of the
pilot/the pilot of
the plane

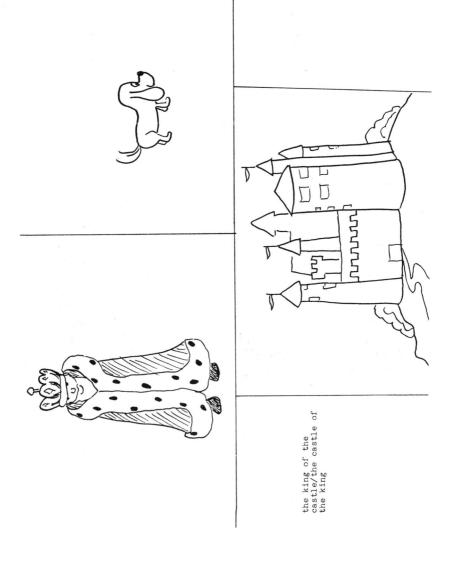

the king of the
castle/the castle of
the king

APPENDIX E

ORDER OF ITEM PRESENTATION IN THE FRENCH,
ENGLISH, AND ACROSS-LANGUAGES TESTS

1. English test

Inflectional categories	Picture chosen		
	1	2	3
1. they write	___	___	___
2. she sees him	___	___	___
3. they open the window	___	___	___
4. the grandfather	___	___	___
5. their dog	___	___	___
6. he buys a ticket	___	___	___
7. the girl	___	___	___
8. he pushes her	___	___	___
9. he is eating	___	___	___
10. his dog	___	___	___
11. the boy	___	___	___
12. he bought a ticket	___	___	___
13. their ball	___	___	___
14. the dog	___	___	___
15. he will buy a ticket	___	___	___
16. he opens the window	___	___	___
17. he writes	___	___	___
18. the books	___	___	___
19. he pushes him	___	___	___
20. he ate	___	___	___
21. he will eat	___	___	___
22. the grandmother	___	___	___
23. the dogs	___	___	___
24. she sees her	___	___	___
25. the book	___	___	___
26. his ball	___	___	___

Syntactic structures

1. the baby on the table is eating the cake
2. the black ball is larger than the white one
3. the boy hits the ball
4. the cat scares the bird which is on the chair
5. the car is longer than the truck
6. the baby sees the girl
7. the baby gives the ball for the dog to the cat
8. the girl is seen by the boy
9. the dog with a big ball
10. the big cat with a bird
11. the boys see each other
12. the pilot of the plane
13. the white ball is larger than the black one
14. the castle of the king
15. the girl brings the ball for the mother to the baby
16. the baby goes from the window to the door
17. the mother brings the dog to the boy
18. the girl shows the cow to the dog
19. the plane of the pilot
20. the baby eats the cake which is on the table
21. the ball hits the boy
    (the boy shows the cat the bird)
22. the girl brings the ball for the baby to the
    mother
23. the boys see themselves
24. the girl gives the ball to the baby
25. the big dog with a ball
26. the cat jumps from the table to the floor
27. the ball is hit by the boy
28. the baby gives the ball for the cat to the dog
29. the girls see each other
30. the baby goes from the door to the window
31. the cat with a big bird
32. the boy brings the cat to the mouse
33. the girl sees the baby
34. the cat on the chair scares the bird
35. the king of the castle
36. the cat jumps from the floor to the table
37. the girl shows the dog to the cow
38. the truck is longer than the car
39. the baby is seen by the girl
40. the baby gives the ball to the girl
    (the boy shows the bird the cat)
41. the boy is hit by the ball
42. the boy brings the dog to the mother
43. the girls see themselves
44. the boy brings the mouse to the cat

Synonymous sentences

1. the truck pushes the car
    (a) the car is pushed by the truck
    (b) the truck is pushed by the car

2. the ball which is white is near the dog
    (a) the white ball is near the dog
    (b) the ball is near the white dog

3. the cat has a ball which is black
    (a) the black cat has a ball
    (b) the cat has a black ball

4. the car is pushed by the truck
    (a) the truck pushes the car
    (b) the car pushes the truck

5. the boy pushes the girl
    (a) the boy pushes her
    (b) the boy pushes him

6. the boy hits the ball
    (a) the ball is hit by the boy
    (b) the boy is hit by the ball

7. I see the castle of the king
    (a) I see the castle
    (b) I see the king

8. the boy is hit by the ball
    (a) the boy hits the ball
    (b) the ball hits the boy

9. I see the pilot of the plane
    (a) I see the plane
    (b) I see the pilot

10. the boy sees the flower
    (a) the boy sees it
    (b) the boy sees her

2. French test

Inflectional categories

Picture chosen

	1	2	3
1. ils écrivent	___	___	___
2. elle le voit	___	___	___
3. ils ouvrent la fenêtre	___	___	___
4. le grand-père	___	___	___

5. leur chien
6. il achète un billet
7. la fille
8. il la pousse
9. il mange
10. son chien
11. le garçon
12. il a acheté un billet
13. leur balle
14. le chien
15. il va acheter un billet
16. il ouvre la fenêtre
17. il écrit
18. les livres
19. il le pousse
20. il a mangé
21. il va manger
22. la grand-mère
23. les chiens
24. elle la voit
25. le livre
26. sa balle

Syntactic structures

1. le bébé sur la table mange du gâteau
2. la balle noire est plus grosse que la blanche
3. le garçon frappe la balle
4. le chat fait peur à l'oiseau qui est sur la chaise
5. la voiture est plus longue que le camion
6. le bébé voit la fille
7. le bébé donne la balle pour le chien au chat
8. la fille est vue par le bébé
9. le chien avec une grosse balle
10. le gros chat avec un oiseau
11. les garçons se regardent les uns les autres
    (la mère montre le livre à la fille pour le garçon)
12. le pilote de l'avion
13. la balle blanche est plus grosse que la noire
14. le château du roi
15. la fille apporte la balle pour la mère au bébé
16. le bébé va de la fenêtre à la porte
17. la mère apporte le chien au garçon
    (la mère montre le livre au garçon pour la fille)
18. la fille montre la vache au chien
19. l'avion du pilote
20. le bébé mange le gâteau qui est sur la table
21. la balle frappe le garçon

22. la fille apporte la balle pour le bébé à la mère _____ _____ _____
23. les garçons se regardent _____ _____ _____
24. la fille donne la balle au bébé _____ _____ _____
25. le gros chien avec une balle _____ _____ _____
26. le chat saute de la table au plancher _____ _____ _____
27. la balle est frappée par le garçon _____ _____ _____
28. le bébé donne la balle pour le chat au chien _____ _____ _____
29. les filles se regardent les unes les autres _____ _____ _____
30. le bébé va de la porte à la fenêtre _____ _____ _____
31. le chat avec un gros oiseau _____ _____ _____
32. le garçon apporte le chat à la souris _____ _____ _____
33. la fille voit le bébé _____ _____ _____
34. le chat sur la chaise fait peur à l'oiseau _____ _____ _____
35. le roi du château _____ _____ _____
36. le chat saute du plancher à la table _____ _____ _____
37. la fille montre le chien à la vache _____ _____ _____
38. le camion est plus long que la voiture _____ _____ _____
39. le bébé est vu par la fille _____ _____ _____
40. le bébé donne la balle à la fille _____ _____ _____
41. le garçon est frappé par la balle _____ _____ _____
42. le garçon apporte le chien à la mère _____ _____ _____
43. les filles se regardent _____ _____ _____
44. le garçon apporte la souris au chat _____ _____ _____

Synonymous sentences

1. le camion pousse la voiture
   (a) la voiture est poussée par le camion
   (b) le camion est poussé par la voiture

2. la balle qui est blanche est près du chien
   (a) la balle blanche est près du chien
   (b) la balle est près du chien blanc

3. le chat a une balle qui est noire
   (a) le chat noir a une balle
   (b) le chat a une balle noire

4. la voiture est poussée par le camion
   (a) le camion pousse la voiture
   (b) la voiture pousse le camion

5. le garçon pousse la fille
   (a) le garçon le pousse
   (b) le garçon la pousse

6. le garçon frappe la balle
   (a) la balle est frappée par le garçon
   (b) le garçon est frappé par la balle

7. je vois le château du roi
   (a) je vois le château
   (b) je vois le roi

8. le garçon est frappé par la balle
   (a) le garçon frappe la balle
   (b) la balle frappe le garçon

9. je vois le pilote de l'avion
   (a) je vois l'avion
   (b) je vois le pilote

10. le garçon regarde la fleur
   (a) le garçon le regarde
   (b) le garçon la regarde

3. Across-languages test

Similar structures

1. le chat a une balle qui est noire
   (a) the cat has a ball which is black
   (b) the cat which is black has a ball

2. le bébé voit la mère
   (a) the mother sees the baby
   (b) the baby sees the mother

3. la mère dit qu'il est dans la cuisine
   (a) the mother says she is in the kitchen
   (b) the mother says he is in the kitchen

4. le garçon la pousse
   (a) the boy pushes him
   (b) the boy pushes her

5. the mother says he is coming
   (a) la mère dit qu'il vient
   (b) la mère dit qu'elle vient

6. the girl sees him
   (a) la fille la voit
   (b) la fille le voit

7. the car which is big pushes the truck
   (a) la voiture qui est grande pousse le camion
   (b) la voiture pousse le camion qui est grand

8. the mother is seen by the baby
   (a) le bébé est vu par la mère
   (b) la mère est vue par le bébé

Syntactic variants

1. la balle frappe le garçon
   (a) the ball is hit by the boy
   (b) the boy is hit by the ball

2. la voiture est poussée par le camion
   (a) the truck pushes the car
   (b) the car pushes the truck

3. la voiture qui est longue pousse le camion
   (a) the car pushes the long truck
   (b) the long car pushes the truck

4. je vois le roi du château
   (a) I see the castle
   (b) I see the king

5. la mère dit que les garçons viennent
   (a) the mother says he is coming
   (b) the mother says they are coming

6. le garçon pousse la fille
   (a) the boy pushes her
   (b) the boy pushes him

7. the car pushes the truck
   (a) la voiture est poussée par le camion
   (b) le camion est poussé par la voiture

8. the mother is seen by the baby
   (a) le bébé voit la mère
   (b) la mère voit le bébé

9. the ball which is white is near the dog
   (a) la balle blanche est près du chien
   (b) la balle est près du chien blanc

10. I see the pilot of the plane
    (a) je vois l'avion
    (b) je vois le pilote

11. the mother says the boy is coming
    (a) la mère dit qu'il vient
    (b) la mère dit qu'elle vient

12. the baby sees the girl
    (a) le bébé la voit
    (b) le bébé le voit

REFERENCES

Barik, H. C. and M. Swain. 1972. Bilingual education project: Interim report on the Spring 1972 testing programme. Toronto, Ontario Institute for Studies in Education.

Bateson, G. 1972. The logical categories of learning and communication. In: Steps to an ecology of mind. San Francisco, Chandler.

Berko, J. 1958. The child's learning of English morphology. Word. 14.150-177.

Bever, T. G. 1970. The cognitive basis for linguistic structures. In: Hayes (1970)

_____. 1971. The integrated study of language behavior. In: Biological and social factors in psycholinguistics. Edited by J. R. Morton. London, Logos.

Bourne, L. E., Jr. and K. O'Banion. 1971. Conceptual rule learning and chronological age. Developmental Psychology. 5.525-534.

Braine, M. D. S. and B. L. Shanks. 1965. The development of conservation of size. Journal of Verbal Learning and Verbal Behavior. 4.227-242.

Brainerd, C. J. 1971. The development of the proportionality scheme in children and adolescents. Developmental Psychology. 5.469-476.

Brown, R. and C. Hanlon. 1970. Derivational complexity and order of acquisition in child speech. In: Hayes (1970).

Bruner, J. S. 1964. The course of cognitive growth. American Psychologist. 19.1-16.

_____, R. R. Olver, and P. M. Greenfield, eds. 1966. Studies in cognitive growth. New York, Wiley.

Ching, D. C. 1969. Reading, language development, and the bilingual child: An annotated bibliography. Elementary English. 46.622-628.

Chomsky, C. 1969. The acquisition of syntax in children from 5 to 10. Cambridge, Mass., MIT Press.

Chomsky, N. 1957. Syntactic structures. The Hague, Mouton.

_____. 1964. Aspects of the theory of syntax. Cambridge, Mass., MIT Press.

_____. 1968. Language and mind. New York, Harcourt.

Clark, E. 1973. What's in a word? In: Cognitive development in the acquisition of language. Edited by T. E. Moore. New York, Academic Press.

Di Pietro, R. J. 1971. Language structures in contrast. Rowley, Mass., Newbury House.

Dulay, H. C. and M. K. Burt. 1972. Goofing: An indicator of children's second language learning strategies. Language Learning. 22.235-252.

Edwards, H. P. and M. C. Casserly. 1973. Evaluation of second language programs in the English schools: Annual report, 1972-73. Ottawa, Ottawa Roman Catholic Separate School Board.

Elkind, D. 1961. Children's discovery of the conservation of mass, weight, and volume: Piaget replication study II. Journal of Genetic Psychology. 98.219-227.

_____. 1964. Discrimination, seriation, and numeration of size and dimensional differences in young children: Piaget replication study II. Journal of Genetic Psychology. 104.275-296.

Ervin, S. M. 1964. Imitation and structural change in children's language. In: New directions in the study of language. Edited by E. H. Lenneberg. Cambridge, Mass., MIT Press.

Fillmore, C. J. 1968. The case for case. In: Universals in linguistic theory. Edited by E. Bach and R. T. Harms. New York, Holt, Rinehart and Winston.

_____. 1971. Some problems for case grammar. In: Georgetown University Round Table on Languages and Linguistics 1971. Edited by Richard J. O'Brien, S. J. Washington, D. C., Georgetown University Press. 35-56.

Fodor, J., M. Garrett, and T. Bever. 1968. Some syntactic determinants of complexity, II: Verb structure. Perception and Psychophysics. 3.453-461.

Francis, H. 1972. Toward an explanation of the syntagmatic-paradigmatic shift. Child Development. 43.949-958.

Fraser, C., U. Bellugi, and R. Brown. 1963. Control of grammar in imitation, comprehension, and production. Journal of Verbal Learning and Verbal Behavior. 2.121-135.

Glucksberg, S., T. Trabasso, and J. Wald. 1973. Linguistic structures and mental operations. Cognitive Psychology. 5.338-370.

Greenfield, P. M. 1966. On culture and conservation. In: Studies in cognitive growth. Edited by J. S. Bruner, R. R. Olver, and P. M. Greenfield. New York, Wiley.

Hayes, J. R., ed. 1970. Cognition and the development of language. New York, Wiley.

Hornby, P. A., W. A. Hass, and C. Feldman. 1970. A developmental analysis of the 'psychological' subject and predicate of the sentence. Language and Speech. 13.182-193.

Hunt, K. W. 1970. Syntactic maturity in schoolchildren and adults. Monographs of the Society for Research in Child Development. 35 (Whole No. 137).

Jakobovits, L. 1970. Foreign language learning: A psycholinguistic analysis. Rowley, Mass., Newbury House.

Katz, J. J. 1964. Mentalism in linguistics. Language. 40.124-137.

Kessler, C. 1969. Deep to surface contrasts in English and Italian imperatives. Language Learning. 19.99-106.

_____. 1971. The acquisition of syntax in bilingual children. Washington, D. C., Georgetown University Press.

King, W. 1966. A developmental study of rule learning. Journal of Experimental Child Psychology. 4.217-231.

Lambert, W. E. and G. R. Tucker. 1972. Bilingual education of children. Rowley, Mass., Newbury House.

Lenneberg, E. H. 1967. The biological foundations of language. New York, Wiley.

Macnamara, J. 1967. The bilingual's linguistic performance: A psychological overview. Journal of Social Sciences. 23. 58-77.

Maratsos, M. P. 1973. Decrease in the understanding of the word 'big' in preschool children. Child Development. 44. 747-752.

McCawley, J. D. 1968. The role of semantics in a grammar. In: Universals in linguistic theory. Edited by E. Bach and R. T. Harms. New York, Holt, Rinehart and Winston.

McNeill, D. 1970. The acquisition of language: The study of developmental psycholinguistics. New York, Harper.

Moerk, E. L. 1973. Specific cognitive antecedents of structures and functions involved in language acquisition. Child Study Journal. 3. 77-90.

Paris, S. G. 1973. Comprehension of language connectives and propositional logical relationships. Journal of Experimental Child Psychology. 16. 278-291.

Peal, E. and W. E. Lambert. 1962. The relation of bilingualism to intelligence. Psychological Monographs. 76 (Whole No. 546).

Piaget, J. 1952. The child's conception of number. London, Routledge & Kegan Paul. First English edition, 1941.

_____. 1964. Cognitive development in children: The Piaget papers. In: Piaget rediscovered: A report of the conference on cognitive studies and curriculum development. Edited by R. E. Ripple and V. N. Rockcastel. Ithaca, New York, Cornell University Press.

_____. 1970. Genetic epistemology. New York, Columbia University Press.

_____. 1971. Biology and knowledge: An essay on the relations between organic regulations and cognitive processes. Chicago, University of Chicago Press.

_____ and B. Inhelder. 1969. The psychology of the child. New York, Basic Books.

_____. 1971. Mental imagery in the child. New York, Basic Books.

Premack, D. 1971. On the assessment of language competence in the chimpanzee. In: Behavior of nonhuman primates. Edited by A. M. Schrier and F. Stollnitz. Vol. 4. New York, Academic Press.

Reber, A. S. 1973. On psycho-linguistic paradigms. Journal of Psycholinguistic Research. 2. 289-319.

Richards, J. A. 1971. A non-contrastive approach to error analysis. English Language Teaching. 24. 204-219.

Rose, S. A. 1973. Acquiescence and conservation. Child Development. 44. 811-814.

Rothenberg, B. B. 1969. Conservation of number among four- and five-year-old children: Some methodological considerations. Child Development. 40. 383-406.

Shipley, E., C. Smith, and L. Gleitman. 1969. A study in the acquisition of language: Free responses to commands. Language. 45. 322-342.

Silverman, I. W. and E. Geiringer. 1973. Dyadic interaction and conservation induction: A test of Piaget's equilibration model. Child Development. 44. 815-820.

Sinclair-de-Zwart, H. 1967. Acquisition du language et développement de la pensée. Paris, Dunod.

_____. 1969. Developmental psycholinguistics. In: Studies in cognitive development. Edited by D. Elkind and J. H. Flavell. New York, Oxford University Press.

Slobin, D. I. 1971. Developmental psycholinguistics. In: A survey of linbuistic science. Edited by W. O. Dingwall. College Park, Md., University of Maryland Linguistics Program.

Sonstroem, A. M. 1966. On the conservation of solids. In: Studies in cognitive growth. Edited by J. S. Bruner, R. R. Olver, and P. M. Greenfield. New York, Wiley.

Swartz, K. and A. E. Hall. 1972. Development of relational concepts and word definition in children five through eleven. Child Development. 43. 239-244.

Tremaine, R. V. 1972. Development of complementation in children's written language. Unpublished Master's thesis presented to the Faculty of Graduate Studies of Carleton University, Ottawa.

Tulving, E. and S. A. Madigan. 1970. Memory and verbal learning. Annual Review of Psychology. 21.437-484.

Vasta, R. and R. M. Liebert. 1973. Auditory discrimination of novel prepositional construction as a function of age and syntactic background. Developmental Psychology. 9.79-82.

Weir, M. W. 1964. Developmental changes in problem-solving strategies. Psychological Review. 71.473-490.

Yamamoto, L. 1964. Bilingualism: A brief review. Mental Hygiene. 48.468-477.